CAN I HAVE IT ALL?

"With the remarkable honesty of her experiences and observations, Anuranjita highlights the unique challenges that shape the lives of women the world over. Her story is an inspirational tale of personal and professional success, and a powerful reminder of what we need to do – both as individuals and as a society – to unleash the full potential of women, so that they can take up their rightful places in our economies and communities."

– **Cherie Blair**, CBE, QC

A FEW WORDS...FOR...
CAN I HAVE IT ALL?

'Women have an incredible inner strength and resilience to overcome the challenges that our patriarchal society poses to them, as is ably demonstrated in this book. Anuranjita's narrative is lucid, relevant and pragmatic for today's woman who plays multiple roles and aspires to have it all. The focus of the book is on every woman who is looking to tap into her convictions and beliefs – whether at home or at work. It brings alive the magic of simple, but powerful, choices women can and must make each and every day, to follow their dreams and realize their true potential.'

Shabana Azmi, *Actor, Social Activist*

'This book will provide you with an insight into the choices that women make at every stage of their life and career. While we all have tough decisions to make, it is remarkable to see how women have to balance their decisions at all times, prioritizing between family and work. Anu, through her own experience, describes these real life nuances at work and home with candor. A must read for young adults, both men and women.'

Pramit Jhaveri, *CEO, Citi India*

'Anyone leading or navigating today's business environment faced with the rapidly changing societal norms will find Can I have it All? an invaluable must read. Kumar rivets us to the pages as she chronicles her journey and choices from a small town in India to the complexities of the world of global corporations. She gives us insight into the thought processes behind her real-life choices, dilemmas and outcomes, as she traverses the challenges of career success, marriage, maternity, and family expectations and traditions. In the conclusion, she shares the attributes and skills one would need to thrive on this journey no matter the choices made-this is truly a guide for us all.'

Henry G. Jackson, *President and Chief Executive Officer, Society for Human Resource Management*

'Can I have it all?' is an engaging chronicle that resonates with the reader at multiple levels. A great read for anyone looking to discover their purpose, reflect upon their choices or simply ignite their courage and conviction. Anuranjita's narration sums up how one's focus to pursue their passion at work can shape their identity with every passing and defining milestone.'

Kalpana Morparia, *CEO, J.P. Morgan, India*

'In today's fast paced world, both men and women have to balance multiple priorities. However, I find that women are often conflicted and feel guilty with regards to balancing their time between personal and professional. Anuranjita's book beautifully illustrates how women have straddled these different worlds, dream big and yet aspire to have all that their hearts desire. More importantly, it unveils the importance of being content with one's choices as they fearlessly pursue their passions and feel fulfilled.'

Anu Agha, *Director, Thermax Limited*

'In her book, 'Can I Have it All', Anuranjita reveals that in every woman's life, there are two key ingredients – confidence and conviction – needed to help satisfy both, her career aspirations, and her responsibilities at home, resulting in the perfect recipe to realizing her dreams. Her insightful narrative will compel every reader to come forth with conviction and work fearlessly as they create their own formula for a fulfilling life.'

Swati A. Piramal, *Vice Chairperson, Piramal Enterprises Limited*

ANURANJITA KUMAR

CAN I HAVE IT ALL?

Trials and Triumphs in a
woman's journey through the
corporate landscape

BLOOMSBURY
NEW DELHI • LONDON • OXFORD • NEW YORK • SYDNEY

ISBN 978 93 859 3642 5
2 4 6 8 10 9 7 5 3 1

Bloomsbury Publishing India Pvt. Ltd
DDA Complex, LSC Building No.4
Second Floor, Pocket C – 6 & 7, Vasant Kunj
New Delhi 110070
www.bloomsbury.com

Typeset by Manmohan Kumar
Printed and bound in India by Gopsons Papers Ltd

To find out more about our authors and books visit www.bloomsbury.com.
Here you will find extracts, author interviews, details of forthcoming
events and the option to sign up for our newsletters.

This book is dedicated to my children Sid and Avni...for their patience, their understanding, their love.

Thank you for coming into my life...thank you for bringing such joy, fun and laughter into my life...for all the time we spent together and the time we could not, but you were always in my thoughts...from Mamma with love !

The Author has pledged her complete proceeds from this book to the Cherie Blair Foundation for Women

CONTENTS

ACKNOWLEDGEMENTS

I would like to thank several people for their guidance – without their support, my journey of authoring this book may not have even commenced.

There were many inflection points in my career. My career journey may not have been as long and fulfilling had it not been for Sandeep my husband, who has not only been an integral part of my life, but encouraged me into professional adventures that I sometimes felt afraid of…his calm and self assured attitude towards our family life has been the corner – stone of the successful journey I experienced. Hand-in-hand we have worked through every challenge life has thrown at us, and there have been plenty. Thank you Kats!

I have learned the invaluable life lessons of tenacity and drive from my mother Dr. Kiran Kumari and the attitude of " never say die" from my father Dr. Ajit Kumar. My parents gave me the confidence to dream big, the space to define my path and trusted my decisions that were sometime hard to fathom! It was their unflinching support during my career that was not only integral to my journey but also kept me going on my path. I would like to express my profound gratitude to them.

Thank you Tooba Modassir for your partnership, I remain indebted to you for sharing my passion in this "Book Project" and supporting me all the way to discover this treasure. You helped me work through each step of it. Without your support I would never have been able to translate my thoughts into this book. I truly cherish our friendship and admire your thoughts for the cause.

The "dream team"... I am grateful for your unconditional support in translating this dream into a reality...this is a group of volunteers who have been committed to the topic and cause of the book and gave their time to propagate it by creating awareness and reach. Each of you made a huge difference. Thank you Asif Zafar Khan, Anantika Kumari, Anisha Ratwani, Bhanu Singhal, Sugandha Agnani, Prateek Roy, Poonam Sharma, Shahin Dastur Jasudha Kirpalani and Debasis Ghosh.

I would like to my express heartfelt gratitude to my team members, both past and present and the Citi colleagues who made my experience so rich and worthwhile. Our time together has provided precious memories that I carry for life.

Very special thanks to Pramit Jhaveri, CEO, Citi India, D Shivakumar – Chairman, CEO, PepsiCo India and, Niren Chaudhary – President – Yum! Restaurants India, for their support, advice and perspective on the topic and future trends!

I am grateful to Abhijit Bhaduri for his support and guidance in this journey. His steer through every step of this project has been of tremendous value.

Finally thanks to the Bloomsbury team for giving me an opportunity to share my thoughts and beliefs with the larger audience through this book.

PREFACE

I am an ordinary woman from a small town in India. With big dreams in my heart, I have a yearning to touch the sky. I'm a simple person, brought up by parents who gave me a modest yet comfortable life, filled with rich learning. I am a happy individual who has seen the trials and tribulations of life and learnt to survive; a rebel who loves change and conforms to norms imbibed and created by myself.

I wish to share my story with women and men who would like to understand the professional journey of an ordinary, small-town woman. These efforts would be worthwhile if I can help someone smile, feel hopeful and optimistic and less lonely when faced with conflicts like I did.

This book intends to capture and share my experiential learning of what I love, that is, life itself. I like to believe that I have lived life to its fullest, despite its ups and downs. These cycles in my personal and professional journey have a significant role to play in the evolution of the person I am today. Both my work and family define me. My identity is linked with what I do, for better or for worse. I focus on what I want to accomplish and that keeps me going even in the toughest of moments.

During my journey, I have had my share of successes and failures, both at home and at work. However it was a sense of hope for the future that kept me going. Whenever faced with a tough situation, I genuinely believed: I can tide over this. Many times the path unfolded before me with ease, and at other times, I had to push myself to the edge. The energy to keep moving against odds was derived from never losing that pure ingredient – **HOPE**. It gave me the reason to fight, to love and to live. It taught me that tomorrow is yet another day which could be filled with the sunshine of happiness. Hope has been the magnet of my life that keeps pulling me forward.

Over a period of time and through intense reflection I began to recognise what gives me joy. It emanates from the smile on my children's face and my husband appreciating my bad cooking just to boost me up a little! Going out with my team-mates for wine after work, advising a colleague about a work-issue, problem-solving for a demanding business stakeholder and sometimes even letting off steam with peers, have been surprisingly therapeutic. Walking on freshly-cut grass gives me joy, eating lunch in the winter sun fills me with happiness, spending time with old friends, remembering all the silly things we did and getting transported back to being a ten-year-old fills me with a child-like excitement! Getting through college, my first job, first pay raise and my first promotion, have all been such special moments. This sense of joy is very personal, very special. I have enjoyed my time as a daughter, a wife, a mother and as a professional. I have tried to mix all of these together and lived on a high of this cocktail called life!

STRUGGLES have shaped me and made me more resilient. They were never pleasant when they crept into my life and wrapped me in a blanket of darkness. I tried to battle them by finding or creating solutions that did not exist, whilst shielding myself with an armour of hope. Sometimes I tried to wash off this momentary feeling of despair through tears and at other times i just went through it with a smile on my face, but I rarely gave up. I kept going. Looking back, these tough moments have been my most valuable lessons and have led me to successes later in life. Every cloud has a silver lining. Embracing failures and struggles with courage actually propelled me further on the path of realising my potential and dreams that I remain eternally grateful for.

Life is often a travel into a galaxy of uncertainty. We are a part of multiple systems and networks at the same time, but we really may not know how deep and far we have to go. Not all events are under our control as there are multiple forces in the universe that work together or sometimes at cross-purposes, leading to outcomes that may be beyond our control, impacting us positively or negatively. Dealing with ambiguity is far easier if you begin to enjoy it! I learnt that when variables are not under your control, it is prudent to prepare for the best scenario and be ready for the worst. Success is also a function of when and how effort meets opportunity. I do believe that in life there is an element of destiny as much as we need to keep focused on our goals. This destiny is not always under our control as we are a part of the larger universe that we were born in; the play between the forces is beyond us. Enjoy the ambiguity; deal with it by befriending it! Have a plan to achieve your goals, seek support, plan for derailments and set your course. You can't really plan for what you can't see, so be gentle with your dreams. Change is the only Constant in life. Just don't stop dreaming!

We are never alone in our journey. The question is, are we moving along with co-passengers that we don't know or is there a network of friends and supporters who we have connected with along the course of the journey? There have been many occasions in my life when I was overwhelmed with problems, unsure of the next step. Everytime I choked on the trials of life and raised my hand out of the water for help, someone was there to grasp it and pull me out. There was always someone, sometimes many, who did not let me sink. Reaching out to people reciprocates feelings of camaraderie. It creates bonds. If your efforts are genuine, they only reap positive connections. Not all people may be similar to us in their mindset, but diversity of thought fosters learning and brings about an awareness of different perspectives. For many, relationships, friendships and trust have similar meaning. Not every relationship has to be at a level of close friendship and complete trust. Life is not black or white, there are shades of grey in between which define the various strands of every relationship. Relationships can be on different planes and we can gain varying levels of support from each of these levels. In my journey, this network, whether personal or professional, has been a key pillar of support.

In life, we all meet some people who support us and others who will not be allies and may marr our path with obsatcles. We may unintentionally cross their path or at times, circumstances may drive us towards them. In earlier days at work, I would get emotional and worked up if my trust was breached, or if I felt that I was let down in some way. Over a period of time I learnt to forgive and let go. I am not a saint and I would forgive people not because I accepted that behaviour or they gained my trust or confidence, I forgave them to be at peace with myself. If I didn't let go of unpleasant memories they would not let me move forward. They would create distractions and my energies would get channelised towards the not-so-important people or activities. I would rather keep my focus on what I need to do while learning from such people and keeping close to them, to ensure I move forward cautiously. Every person in your life teaches you something. I also learnt to forgive myself for not being a perfect parent or a partner or employee. Recognising your efforts and moving along is the key. You can do what you can do! Too often we are too harsh on ourselves and maybe we just need to celebrate our achievements a bit more!

Commitment is the binding force for what you really want to do. It keeps you focused in trying times and does not let you waiver. Without the constant nourishment of commitment, our dreams can never be nurtured. It is similar to the unconditional love of a mother for her children that really enables her to give more than her hundred percent. For me, commitment came more easily, when I truly liked what I did. It aligned with my values and my soul. Commitment also brought in determination. This enabled me to do things I truly loved. There are commitments towards work goals in my life and there are some key goals that I am truly passionate about at home. It is this sense of strong belief and conviction in my purpose, my goals and relationships that has kept me strongly bound to them. You need to really want something so much that it fosters the strong commitment that drives the effort to make it yours, against all odds. Moreover, without being selfish, we also need to have a commitment to ourselves to be happy!

My relationships define me and some are the very core of my existence. We play multiple roles at the same time, be it at home or at work. We have formal and informal relationships. Some of these demand sacrifices while others are obligations. Balancing all this at the same time requires tough love. Many times we take decisions that are not always ideal, but they will be optimal keeping in mind the larger picture and the multiplicity of goals that we are trying to achieve. When we make choices there is the joy of getting something but also the pain of losing what we let go of. Balancing relationships at home and work is a delicate balance wherein the brain and heart may not always be aligned. Many-a-time we have to be pragmatic, which may be tough and stressful in a few relationships in the short term, but if we believe in our larger purpose in the long term, it all evens out.

Lastly, the fuel for all of the above is positive thinking. In the roller-coaster of life, it is far easier to get stuck with adverse thoughts. Thoughts are contagious and we become what we think. This tends to reflect in our behaviour and attitude. Many times I reached crossroads in life and felt out of control not knowing what the future would be. Anxious feelings can be overwhelming. In such situations thinking of positive outcomes and more importantly, believing in them helped me tide over the crisis. Sometimes I feel, because I believed in them so intensely, I almost forced that positive thinking into outcomes!

My thoughts, feelings and achievements alluded to here, stand on the strong foundation of seven pillars:

- Clarity
- Conviction
- Choices
- Courage
- Confidence
- Connections
- Collaboration

These pillars have steered me through my life and I continue to derive strength from each of them. They carried the load of what I desired and what I wanted. I wanted it all in life...don't we all? With a bit of help and support, I have had it all! Question is what is this 'ALL'?

INTRODUCTION
Climbing the corporate ladder

Dream it.
Believe it.
Achieve it. – World Changing Women@WomenOfHistory

Climbing the corporate ladder is thrilling, exciting, heady, sometimes tough, but it is always enthralling! It has been a topic of debate and discussion for anyone who has ever had a brush with power-play at work. The degree of aspiration may vary or the drivers may differ, but the sense of growth and desire for self actualization is attractive for every individual. Even if you don't wish to embark upon this journey yourself, chances are that you do admire and respect someone who strove hard to make it to the top. And this is because the journey is never easy!

Isn't it then quite obvious that this journey should touch women as much the same way as men…think not? Why? And if yes, then why does breaking the glass ceiling or encouraging diversity still remain a challenge for every organisation? Why do discussions related to increasing representation by the 'fairer sex' still seem so new and relevant?

Climbing the corporate ladder for women means completing this journey through a different route – and a comparatively tougher one, so say statistics. According to recent reports from Catalyst (a non-profit organisation working to expand opportunities for women in business), about 19.2 per cent of the board seats of S&P500 companies, are held by women. Further, women CEOs are still a minority holding 4.8 per cent of CEO positions at S&P 500 companies (Catalyst. *2014 Catalyst Census: Women Board Directors.* New York: Catalyst, 2015). C-Suite numbers too reflect a number ranging from eighteen to twenty per cent in various recent researches. These numbers are fairly small and growing at a much slower pace even though the percentage of women graduating from professional institutes has grown over the last decade. Women are ahead of men in their report cards and academic achievements but yet get paid less. In some countries, even up to sixty per cent of graduates are women. However more men tend to focus on the sciences – technology, engineering and mathematics (STEM) while women gravitate towards less lucrative degrees in humanities.

What makes this journey different for women? Or is it really different? Can gender alone, make so much difference – and that too, in the corporate world?

I don't know all the answers, but having traversed a sizeable length of this journey, I do feel that being a woman dictates the course. The climb is different even though the destination is the same. Ultimately it all depends on your own desire, on what 'I' want, that determines the success. And 'I' is gender-neutral.

REFLECTIONS

Standing at the crossroads again today – much calmer, more peaceful than ever before, I decide on the next step in my life. Nostalgia creeps in. Four decades have passed by, and I am a mother of two beautiful children, yet I continue to feel like a child. How time has flown! Sitting here at the Hong Kong airport looking at the gigantic aircraft, peering inside to woo passengers, I contemplate upon my past. These aircrafts were intimidating,

like the corridors of power at work, where we were also trying
to bond with new employees...getting to know them better.
Airports have become my home and these airplanes my friends.
I do not mind this life. However, sometimes this travel does get
ahead of me...for now I sit here calm and peaceful, looking back
at the decades that have passed by...some existential questions
start creeping into my head and my thoughts start to cloud...I
look at my watch and there are two hours to go for my flight, so
I settle snugly in the corner sofa chair with a coffee, reflecting
and writing my thoughts down.

As I think about what is next for me in life at work, I start to
wonder where I am with my current role at Citi. Have I broken
the glass ceiling? By taking the road less travelled at different
milestones in my life, have I reached where I wanted to be?
The more I think, the more at ease I feel. I am not sure if I have
reached my destination (I wish I knew what that was!) but it feels
I am on a track that I aspire to be on and need to keep prodding
along. So how do I commence my next innings and what would
it take for me to get there?

I close my eyes and my whole life flashes before me. I can
feel a child-like excitement at my mother's home. Her warm
hands caressing my hair, school anxiety, scorn for a few and
love for a many, the excitement at my first day at work, my
first recognition, promotion, marriage, motherhood...so
much has passed by and I truly feel more holistic than ever,
completely ready to bat out my next innings! There's celebration
and cheer of having accomplished something. Yet, I feel the
hunger and excitement towards what an uncertain future may
hold for me !

What is the next innings in leadership? The answer is a bit
hazy but also mysteriously exciting...it is the familiar feeling I
experience at every milestone of my professional life every few
years. The time spent reflecting helps me relax and the clouds
part away gradually.

Life has been a roller-coaster ride with its highs and lows. I have enjoyed this journey, emerging as a slightly different, more rounded individual after each ride. My early experiences shaped my values, perspectives and drivers which kept me on course when I entered the corporate world, which was not an easy place for a woman a few decades ago. But now, two decades later, though it's relatively easier for women to get to the top, I feel may be I was fortunate to ride the wave.

My reflections and my learnings that have helped shape me, my personal and professional life, are captured for you. If this can help any woman in any way to propel her career forward, my journey would become more meaningful and rich. We all start similar. What matters is what you manage to make of it.

With this book I hope to make a small difference towards that change and provide others with the perspectives and learnings that I have gathered in my journey. As Hillary Clinton is known to have said, 'When it comes to the enormous challenge of our time, to systematically and relentlessly pursue more economic opportunity in our lands, we don't have a person to waste and we certainly don't have a gender to waste.'

1 CLARITY OF PURPOSE

helps us move through the passage of time in the right direction! As the famous Cheshire cat stated, 'If you don't know where you want to go, then any road will take you there'

CLARITY OF PURPOSE

The purpose of one's life can't possibly go beyond achieving your greatest self and recognising what this self can really do! Thus, it does become imperative to find out what this self is capable of, and how and where it may be discovered, so that we can then engage in maximising its potential. Introspections and reflection can find and refine this self.

I believe a lot of it lies in your growing years, when you are forming the first impressions about the world, trying to figure out within yourself, your own little space. A few aha! moments. A few eureka moments that gradually create a trail for us to follow and give us some idea about our destination.

I come from a modest family where my parents earned enough to provide a comfortable life for us two sisters. My father completed his PhD and took up a job at a pharmaceutical company in a small town called Rishikesh. My mother, a fairly driven lady, is a gynaecologist from a well-known, Indian medical college.

While my father, a humble man, ensured we remained grounded, my mother, a driven professional and a very far-sighted, proactive woman, ensured we were well-prepared to deal with the big, bad world.

My mother always pushed the edge on risky decisions, which was quite contrary to my conservative father's style. But it would somewhat serve as a perfect balance in the house on how we did things as a family. We were two sisters with me being the older one. My grandmother was of the view that my mother should have been supported by a son.

My mother always believed that her daughters could be her sons. At that age I was not sure what that was supposed to mean but as I grew up it became apparent that it implied someone who was more capable of having a great job, status and wealth! I often debated why I could not be slated to earn all that even as a daughter? My mother raised us like her sons, which at that time was difficult for me to decipher but as I became more worldly-wise I figured it out. I kept on questioning why I needed to be a boy to achieve all of that.

We were a typical, Indian family with a high premium on education; my parents were very ambitious about the quality of education that they wanted their children to have. The fact that my parents were highly-educated meant the children were expected to exceed in the space as well. Rishikesh being a small town with limited quality schools, I was sent to a premium boarding school, Welhams, in Dehradun, at the age of seven. I don't have many memories apart from the night when my mother left me in the boarding and I ran frantically behind her while my teachers held me back. I could see my mother's tears rolling down her cheeks but her steps were unwavering towards the exit of the school, as she knew tears today will toughen me up to weather the storms of tomorrow.

THE SEEDS OF SELF-RELIANCE ARE SOWN

My years in boarding taught me early decision-making and self-reliance. At Welhams, I met children from a wide range of backgrounds ranging from royalty to political families, from wealthy backgrounds to grounded middle-income homes. School was wonderful and tried its best to keep social disparity at bay. There were kinder girls, not-so-kind girls, collaborators, and friends...and some opportunistic peers. Given we were away from our families, our emotional needs were fulfilled through the bonds with teachers, friends and matrons. Welhams School was a true reflection of the real world; it was like growing up in a lab, which was fully simulated to reflect the trials and tribulations of the real world.

I vividly recall our transition from junior school to senior school as a real landmark. We were suddenly designated as grown-ups yet we were the junior-most batch amongst the senior girls. Cozy rooms transformed into never-ending, large dormitories. Some seniors led the way to settle us in, whereas others would be distant till their kinder side would surface and they would befriend you. We scurried around to figure out what this new phase of our school life had in store for us: more studies, extra-curricular, sports, outings on our own and so on. It was exciting and challenging at the same time. The path was for you to discover and the support of teachers and buddies was always available. At times it was easier if you knew the right seniors to crack the code to the new environment...somewhat similar to our workplace in current times. It was a true reflection of how our work environment works with constant change, relationships and play. One had to be determined to win, push oneself and work one's way around! I learnt a great deal about how to think and execute, during these transitions...much more than was ever taught in any textbook.

We were completely self-reliant when it came to studies, no parents or tuitions to help; you could reach out to teachers, seniors or friends. Hence a strong sense of self awareness and drive was extremely critical. We became what we intended to be...there was no one to push us onto any prescribed path as the path had to be decided by oneself. It was truly a foundation I cherish as it was to hold me in good stead for many years to come. It ignited a fire in me to do something bigger. At this stage of my life, I was unclear how this would pan out. However, the little green shoots were sprouting. I just wanted to be somebody worthwhile!

Twenty five years after graduating from school, I can say that I am that somebody I feel happy about. Recently, when I met my entire batch of the class of 1989 at the Silver Jubilee reunion, I felt a sense of jubilant hysteria. It was wonderful to see everybody and we were transported back to the old days in school. Each had chartered a different course of life for herself, all very beautiful, but only some chose to pursue a full time career. I noticed how many of us had gone into completely divergent paths of being homemakers, consultants, artists, professionals and so on, inspite of a similar foundation…it is the path all of us chose, or in some cases our families chose, (if we were not clear)…that now defined us. I have to confess what was evident was that of all the girls who graduated together, a larger percentage chose to be caregivers… were these choices made consciously? Were they circumstantial? Or maybe it did not matter? I was privileged to have some very talented girls in my class and selfishly I wished to have more of them with me, hand in hand, in this corporate jungle. We were and would have been a formidable team!

A TEST OF SELF-BELIEF

I grew up trying to be more than just a 'girl child' in a country where a boy child is still a preferred option (as if there could be one!). I often witnessed my parents being told in passing discussions amongst relatives about how they have to save up to get two girls settled (politely meant marriage) and how it would have been better if one of us had been a boy. I despised such discussions and it somehow egged me on to create a deeper impact. The rebel in me was gradually and constructively growing.

Driven by my desire to create an impact that would fulfil my mother's dream to have another doctor in the family, like a good, Indian student I studied math and science to enable me to appear for medical exams. I secured admission in a top-league medical college. Given my mother's wish and I, being the older one, felt obliged to fulfil her desire. But a few months in college and it became apparent that something was not right. I was unhappy and not settling into the seemingly studious and different environment. Contemplating over the first few weeks made me realise that medicine is not something I was actually interested in. I had taken the subject only for my mother and for all the negative comments that she had to face for the two daughters she had...the dilemma was evident. I felt stifled in classrooms, with classmates who were culturally very different from what I had been used to at Welhams. A part of me was dying every day and the conviction that this was not my purpose, grew strong. A couple of months later, when I spoke to my parents, they were truly shocked. It was fairly difficult for them, especially my mother, to understand why I would want to give up studying medicine (admissions for which are very difficult in the college I went to) and charter out into an unknown future! My father was calmer about it and let me take charge only on one condition: I needed to secure alternate admission in a good university.

Faced with this self-created crisis, the flames of my earlier kindled purpose to make an impact, grew stronger, I felt I had let my parents down in some way by this episode and wanted to find a solution. I was responsible for the outcome and felt fully engaged towards resolving it. In October, 1989, I went from college to college in Delhi University begging for a seat. However, knowing fully well the competition amongst students in Delhi, I had to tell myself every morning that it would be fine. I had to make myself really believe this – as sometimes the seeds of doubt would creep in. I had no options, so keeping optimistic was my only panacea. After tremendous persistence I got admission in one college with hostel promised after a month. Apart from the admission, the hostel situation was critical as I had no one to live with in Delhi. I knew my parents would not let me live by myself given their view of the safety and security situation in Delhi. As they say, sometimes when you want something so intensely the whole universe conjures it all up to give it to you! I felt something like that happened here. It was the best college for the subject I chose: Psychology! Phew...! I was grateful for the strength and determination that I had garnered in school to tide me through this phase.

FOLLOWING MY HEART

Victoriously I apprised my parents that I had landed myself in a college under Delhi University and that too with an honours in psychology, a specialisation it was known for. Even though it was a subject I knew nothing about but something felt right this time. I saw no reason to pursue the sciences if I was not going to make a career out of it. My parents were both inclined to the sciences and they thought humanities as an area not reliable enough to secure one a prospective career, were evidently shocked ! But they remained calm, veiling their disappointment even though I could sense the lack of excitement and joy on their faces that had been apparent when they'd heard about medical school. A pain seared through my heart...have I disappointed them? Will I make it up? Will I be able to create an impact? Am I doing this right? After all they had more experience than I had. Should I believe in myself to take a leap of faith? Then it struck me that if I can't take a leap of faith myself...who will? I decided I have to make this work even though I was unsure what psychology would lead me to.

I moved to Delhi, commenced my degree and fell in love with the subject. I realised great teachers and mentors make a big difference. Unlike school, where teachers treated us like children (as we were!), college opened my mind and more mature relationships with professors transformed my worldview. I embraced every aspect of the subject from social, child and criminal psychology, various approaches, experiments, and best of all abnormal psychology, which came with a warning. With the introduction of each new chapter we studied in abnormal psychology, we had the feeling that these specific conditions existed within us! Scared and anxious, we thanked our stars to further find that they existed in each individual and it's the extremes that create the problem. However, our professors held us together as they had seen many such mad hatters pass through their lecture rooms. Anyway, I loved the subject as it taught me how each of us stores multi-faceted aspects of our personality, in a disguised way. It was great fun to unravel the amazing mysteries of the human mind.

In retrospect, I'd say psychology was the right decision, the subject, and my mind and heart were aligned, which led to a wonderful outcome, and I was a gold medalist for three straight years. Given what I had let go in medical school and the unspoken expectations of my parents, I felt an over-arching need to prove myself. During those three years I focused only on college studies, with limited interactions and social life. I had some great friends but I used my time much more wisely as I saw it as an investment to earn a great future!

I immersed myself passionately into the subject. I began to believe that this was what I wanted to the specialise in. I contemplated the future and started to plan to go to the United States for further studies. But destiny had something else in store for me.

In retrospect, the college experience made me realise that when you give yourself fully to what you really like, you can get more than hundred per cent returns. The passion for what you love to do so much, transforms that work / study into a fulfilling feeling that leads to rewards beyond what you may have asked for. I learnt the value of relentless focus, ability to zoom in and out of a situation and acquired in-depth knowledge of my favourite theories of Gestalt or systems that I leverage till date. This purpose of making an impact in life got more refined though the milestones were fuzzy and the future a bit hazy...but it was taking form behind those clouds.

WONDERS OF AN OPEN MIND

During my third year of college, as stated earlier, I was planning to go to the US to pursue further studies. I worked through months to do my diligence, applications, ran around every information centre in Delhi for guidance, when one of my professors, Mrs Kapoor, whom I respected the most, called me in for a chat. What was to follow was going to change the course of my life forever.

Oblivious to this, I was looking forward to meeting Mrs. Kapoor that winter evening in Delhi. Surprisingly, in spite of the biting cold, the day felt fresh and the sun shone magically with a glint of warmth on the green grass carpets of our college. I had put together a file of all my applications, college documents, recommendations and details that explained how much I wanted to discuss with Mrs. Kapoor that evening. I was also looking forward to the lovely ginger tea that she always offered when we visited her home. I simply loved the way she prepared that special cup of tea, served with some cookies.

I picked up my file at five in the evening and hurriedly walked towards Mrs Kapoor's house which was at the other end of the college. Clearly, I was keen to maximise every minute of my time with her. She was the Head of the Department and someone who had supported and mentored me as I worked on my grades.

Mrs Kapoor greeted me with a calm smile and then we both sank into comfortable chairs in her living room. The delicious ginger tea arrived with smoke curling over the cup, enticing me to pick it up without any hesitation. I started to update Mrs Kapoor on where I was with my application process. Till then, it had not dawned on me as to why she had really called me there, until she interrupted me after ten minutes and requested me to hold these thoughts. It left me a bit perplexed. She really couldn't be talking about final exams which were almost four months away. Mrs Kapoor lowered her cup of tea on the table and looked at me with a radiant smile.

'Anu, I am so ecstatic to see the passion that you have for this subject. Which part of psychology really excites you?'

'Mrs. Kapoor, I like all of the strands, but clearly the industrial, criminal and abnormal, stand out for me!' I said. This was also evident in my grades and she was well aware of it.

'Hmmm…there is a similarity in all these three strands… you are rectifying something that is broken whilst building on new concepts. All require mind power and tend to have an impact on behaviour and functioning of the human mind by being reactive and proactive at the same time.' She continued, 'The other strands of psychology are more developmental and far more long-term in nature.'

Now I was really confused about where this was all going. Yes, I liked these subjects and would have probably specialised in industrial if I went overseas.

Mrs Kapoor continued, 'Anu, you have a commercial mind that thinks and executes at the same time. I have looked at your MBTI scores and a few more diagnostics. In my view, you are ready to get into the commercial world wherein you can leverage your education in psychology. One of the upcoming, emerging streams in India is Business Education. I am not sure you have thought it through.'

I was now extremely confused as I had not studied Commerce or Economics that would typically be the subjects that lead people from Delhi University into an MBA course. The discussions continued and Mrs. Kapoor turned the thought-reflection mirror towards me, sharing how she had seen me excel in certain topics and enjoy certain experiments. She continued and said that she had noticed my ability to connect psychology to the corporate world at large and not just social work. She encouraged me to think about Management in light of the impact I wanted to create, fuelled by my self-reliance and that feisty drive to get out there and do different things. I walked away after a couple of hours slightly clearer and slightly confused but convinced. I knew I needed to give management a shot, while I concurrently apply to the US universities.

As destiny would have it, or maybe Mrs Kapoor saw something that I couldn't…I took the Common Admission Test (CAT) and got calls from various business schools, including a few IIMs, XLRI and FMS. Post-discussion with the faculty (and of course Mrs Kapoor) I decided to go to XLRI and specialise in HR as that would help me leverage my learnings and groom me for the corporate world.

I realised the value of having an open mind and the willingness to evaluate options objectively. Given how this lesson changed the course of my life, I hold it very dear and practise it to the hilt, even to this day.

ONE BOLD STEP LEADS TO ANOTHER

It was a beautiful monsoon morning when I woke up in the Beldi club in Jamshedpur. The light breeze gently kissed my face welcoming and preparing me for what was in store. My parents had come to drop me to Xaviers Labour Relations Institutes (XLRI) and I looked again hopelessly at the three bulky suitcases

I was carrying. I had given up on explaining to my mother why I did not need so many things anymore. I just wanted to let her rejoice that finally her rebellious, deviant daughter was probably taking her life a little more seriously than she had thought.

My parents did not know much about Management leave alone Human Resources. Management Education was becoming as fashionable in those days, as probably e-commerce is today. A few friends of my parents had affirmed my decision, which had been a big relief for them. They were further assured by the fact that most students from this college got decent jobs irrespective of what they did there!

We entered the XLRI main gate. The campus seemed quaint yet cosy. There was a calming scent of fresh, wet soil from the rain showers overnight. The trees looked washed and the flowers smiled at us, welcoming us to the XLRI campus. There was something about the place that I took an instant liking to and it has stayed with me for a lifetime.

I settled in the girls' hostel with one of my batchmates; classes began, seniors arrived and we gradually settled into the routine, studies, and the ways of the professors, etc.

Business school campuses usually operate in a world of their own. A happy bubble that we lived in for two years and I enjoyed every moment of it from the day I entered campus to the day we had our final farewell party.

The big difference for me was the motley group of people I met and I learnt from. It was not always about what we learnt in the class but a lot more about what we learnt off classes in the dining hall, music room and walking in the garden or while sitting with friends under the *Bodi* tree. Doing project work late at night over the most tasty Maggi, fried in tomato and onion, egg *bhurji* and ginger tea! Those precious moments are stored in my treasured memoirs forever.

There were of course many romantic plays in the works and our batch was much more diverse with more women students. Hence, it was furiously poached by the senior batch for possible matches.

Here is where I found my partner, Sandeep, who was a senior and, at the onset, very different from me, both socially and intellectually. An engineer from Indian Institute of Technology (IIT) was not really my idea of a life partner! We spent some time among friends and our relationship blossomed from thereon. I realised we were different but complemented each other well.

My business school education taught me social skills and the agility to flex my style with very different people. Many of our peers were engineers and probably far more analytical and quick on their feet than I was! A few peers from Mumbai University and Delhi University always lagged behind these geeks in grades and of course, attendance! Students in the class had enrolled from almost more than a dozen states; you could see cliques forming depending on cultural or social background. During this period I learnt to deal with people from varied backgrounds, managed them, made friends with some and stayed away from some. Maybe my psychology background helped me read the undertones and unsaid messages.

Another important feature during this phase was peer learning. As much as there were relevant topics discussed in the class with professors, a lot of the learning really took place from peers and classmates. Various debates, teamwork (sometimes lack of it) during assignments, understanding each other's perspectives, sometimes agreeing with diverse thoughts and sometimes disagreeing with them – made my mind grow and helped me develop a different perspective that broadened my mind.

I could feel that after the stress of college we were beginning to come into our own. It gave us empowerment and autonomy of execution on our careers. Not that decision-making for me was an issue since school or college, XLRI however, taught me considerate decision-making for the right impact, weighing and analysing issues and outcomes, rather than jumping to conclusions at the spur of the moment. It taught me to respect and manage constructively the challenges thrown at you by peers, without getting negative about it.

I felt better and stronger every day!

XLRI also taught us how to enjoy our work. It taught us how you can have fun (and romance) with friends on campus, working on building our future brick-by-brick, while completing our course. We worked hard and we played hard. Our campus was an oasis in Jamshedpur and there was very little to do off-campus, so we all seemed very contained in our little world as if nothing else existed.

As we built our perspective my purpose to make an impact, make a difference and be somebody distinct to my family, strengthened even further. As a small child in Rishikesh, I used to play with friends in a big garden at my mother's hospital. Very often, when we spotted a helicopter or an aircraft in the sky, we used to run after it till we reached the edge of the garden hoping one day we could fly in one of those. Fly we did two decades later...so much so that there has been no looking back. XLRI provided me with the wings to fly.

My purpose got further refined with how to do things and I tightened my seat belt to take my first fight on my final placement day post the two-year course, in January, 1994! XLRI had provided me with the much-needed network, access to learning and confidence, which would be a coveted treasure in the times to come.

As any business school graduate will share with you, the two-year joyful ride ends with a traumatising placement process. The countdown to this moment is built over months with the placement committee working furiously with various companies, to ensure the best roles to open up on campuses which we had to compete for. However, it is a socialistic process wherein the institute wants all students placed; hence, there are very complicated rules about ranking of companies and days of placement. Things like – how many offers can be placed by companies and how many offers a student can expect and so on, came into play. The whole ranking of companies on Day Zero, Day One and so on, had put tremendous pressure on the students. If one was not placed on Day One, it implied that particular student was probably not as good! In a typical Indian competitive student environment this process won hands down.

I never liked this process and would have much preferred that a student be allowed to appear for any company and get as many offers. No company would hire a sub-optimal candidate and no student would gather tens of offers and take none! I clearly lost this battle then. Even to this day when I visit campuses for hiring fresh grads, the process that existed two decades back, still prevails! God bless the young students who go through this!

After much toil, I had a few offers and I chose a top FMCG, because of the brand, track record in people-practice and their new renewed focus in India then. They offered me an opportunity to do something futuristic and I felt I could make a difference and thus create an impact. Little did I realise that I was also creating a rupture in my marital prospects.

Sandeep, who had graduated a year earlier, was already placed with a leading FMCG. But what we hadn't realised by then was that there could be a potential conflict that could arise with us working for competitor companies.

This company was my first brush with corporate experience and a very memorable one at that. I made some deep and wonderful connections with the group of management trainees. We all grew together as professionals. Living on our own, spending our own money – was a significant expression of freedom. Some of those relationships remain with me till date and are very precious. In the corridors of the company head office, I had met my first managers who taught me the nuts and bolts about not just work but also the appropriate behaviours in a professional environment. This company had a very structured approach in "success transferring" best practices across the world, which was immensely useful for young professionals like us, who were ready to assimilate any learning that came our way.

MOVING FORWARD

It is not always easy to plan for an unforeseen future; however, having a view on a larger purpose defines your life as it did mine. I have always worked towards adding value to myself and to the environment around me to progress further. I wanted to be remembered as someone who made a difference. With this purpose somewhat defined, I was able to synchronise my life, interests, energy in the direction of value addition. Milestones were set, some achieved and some not, but I never lost my direction.

Through school and college, I understood that a belief about your purpose that is driven by your values, will create a sense of clarity and conviction that can be unwavering. Clarity of purpose is thus the key not only to achieve, but to stay focused and steady on a path to self-discovery if you take a dive into your mind. It will help you surmount any obstacle and keep you on the right path even though the odds are against it. This is what helped me manage through the tricky decision about my higher education and choice of profession. A clear sense of purpose provides a long term view in such situations and pulls you along. Keep fanning this drive as there will be odds that can pull you down.

SUMMARY

Someone once said that happiness is when you are not striving for it. And more often, every time you live a purpose that isn't your own, this struggle would continue. Be nice to yourself, for you deserve everything that you want. Sometimes you only need the clarity of thought to say 'what I want' first to yourself and then to others. You'd be amazed then to see how just one moment of truth has the potential to simplify your struggles.

Very candidly, so far, my life had progressed like any other girl with a similar background like mine. Not very different. Maybe not even very defining. But, if we look at it again carefully, the desire to succeed had already started to take roots in my life. Key learnings were:

- Outline your purpose: This could be in broader terms the impact you want to create or which direction you want your life to take. Without this defined, we may as well live somebody else's purpose or life. My purpose was to make a difference for the better for people around me in anything I do.

- Follow your heart: 'Feel' your purpose. Choose your own path for your destination. My desire/purpose lent me the courage to decide how. If it did not feel right, then it probably wasn't! That's how I decided to forego medicine for psychology.

- Strong sense of purpose will lead to your convictions, which is the key to taking this journey forward. You simply need to know what *you* want! It will also help you to think things through and clear any hurdles that may come in your way. This is the real foundation for what you may want to achieve in life; personally or professionally. Hence, it is imperative that the foundation is strong, as your life-long dreams can get transformed into realities based on this.

While one's destiny decides where one is born and consequently the education and upbringing, there is definitely more than that which contributes to how one's life evolves. So what is it? Maybe your purpose is yet to be found. The beauty is that *you* are *always* free to choose your purpose, a better future, anytime.

2 CONVICTION
is the belief that enables persistence

CONVICTION

'Nothing will work unless you do.'
– Maya Angelou

DIP IN CORPORATE WATERS

Knowing what you want and being passionate about the work you do differentiates between the good and the great. Caught amidst different roles, women are sometimes unsure and feel guilty of what they want professionally. Once you have the clarity of purpose, comes the conviction of thought and the plan to execute. Be it a new role or a transfer, to be effective, one needs to be disciplined and be prepared in advance. Finally, conviction is the virtue that lets you accomplish all that you plan for. After all, Rome was not built in a day! It has worked for me because when you take risks, odds cannot be avoided and it is that constant inner mantra that keeps playing inside your head: 'believe in yourself'. This not only encourages you to continue on your journey but also finally leads you to your destination.

Be it a man or a woman – climbing the corporate ladder is not easy for either. It is fraught with a lot of excitement and also with quite a few challenges. To remain on the path, you need to be clear, focused and passionate about what you want out of life and how strongly you want it. Then, get ready for the ride with a lot of energy and passion and push yourself towards the goal that you have set for yourself.

So, to get ready for the race, bear in mind that this is not a hundred-metre sprint, but a long marathon which will last for years. You need to pace yourself out, be ready to spend your energy and keep yourself focused towards the goal post. Pace your race!

A word of caution: It will not always be possible to plan for all the changes on the way, speed bumps and the highs and lows of this ride. However, having an eye on the final destination will define your journey and keep your life on track, as it did mine.

Sometimes flexing your path, taking a detour, especially in changed circumstances, maybe the right call so long as it is tied to your larger purpose which is not event-bound. This is what I finally did when I changed my plan of going to the US for further education and stayed back in India to pursue business education. I changed my path and headed to the right destination.

As stated earlier, I always focused on doing a value addition to the people and environment around me that helped me to add to myself and progress further. At work, value creation is the way I conducted my business and self. I would strategise, problem-solve, execute, reflect and review on how we could make this better. Fortunately for me, a larger purpose in life coincided with my work interests and possibly that made the ride slightly easier.

A BELIEF IN WHAT YOU WANT

A belief in what you want to do, driven by your values, which has evolved with your experiences will create a sense of unwavering conviction to do things. Keep searching for your beliefs. Introspect. Search for the values in your heart. This drives my sense of conviction, especially when each experience validates my purpose. If the actions validate the purpose, it creates a state of happiness and fulfilment. If not, then one may want to reflect on and revisit the purpose or associated actions.

My experience taught me later in life how this belief drove my purpose and also propelled my will to achieve and excel. We are all aware of this fact intellectually but how often do you ask yourself *what really matters? What are your values?* It is amazing how much we don't know about the unconscious self. During my lifetime, I have worked the other way around. Many times when I have felt very strongly about a certain goal or experienced an overwhelming sense of emotion to achieve something; I spoke to myself to understand myself better. It has been pleasantly surprising to find the truth about my drivers and conviction. Conviction is the key to not only achieve and remain focused, but it is also a path to self-discovery. It will help you surmount any obstacles and keep you on the right path even though the odds may seem against it. My advice is to keep fuelling your conviction from time to time, by strengthening your ideas and beliefs to ensure that you *are* on the right path.

MILESTONE TO MILESTONE MAKES THE JOURNEY

Your conviction is a strong anchor that keeps you focused on actions to achieve your purpose. However, the purpose is usually long-term and sometimes lifelong as we discover while growing up. There are goalposts in life that keep us on track. School, college, jobs, family are a part of the journey that forms a part of our larger purpose. Purpose can be long-term but goalposts, in my view, will need to be short to medium term, so that we have some reasonable feedback about how we are progressing on our journey. Convictions are these beliefs that keep us moving from one milestone to another.

As I learnt in the corporate world over a period of time we can have a desire to be in the C-suite. However, what gets us there will need to be planned and measured progressively every twelve to twenty four months from the onset of your career.

CROSSROADS AND THE WILL TO GO ON

India is unique in many ways. Ironically, several studies have placed urban workforce participation of women as low as thirteen per cent, while the rural participation tends to be higher at about thirty per cent, probably due to the absolute necessity for women to work in rural areas to maintain a subsistence level. Ideally, one would imagine that, more women in the cities are stepping out to work! Also, while there are several initiatives running for increasing education levels among women, numbers of women in eductaional institutes have increased but a staggering proportion choose not to work, even after earning a degree. As income levels are rising in cities, workforce participation of women is surprisingly dropping! We are truly a country of many complexities with cultural conditioning playing a huge role in these outcomes.

I have seen so many bright, independent women abandon their careers easily and instantly, with marriage or maternity being one of the most common drivers. Is this a matter of choice or a lack of conviction to carry on in the face of life taking a new turn? And not just corporate careers; there are so many examples of women in the performing arts or film industry who simply stop working once they are married. In India, actresses from the big league suddenly become less popular after their marriage. Is this a common mindset or an erosion of convictions?

Sometimes this occurs because the decision to work is driven by *need* rather than *desire*. Once economically and socially secure in their marriage, the conviction to work, especially as perceived by others suddenly drops!

In a work life of a woman, there are usually three common crossroads wherein women are challenged to take key decisions in regard to their career. Tiding over these crossroads requires a huge amount of conviction in what she wants and how she wishes to make it work.

1. Marriage: Most South Asian women grow up and are conditioned to think about marriage as a key milestone and not just a key event in life. This is also driven by a generic expectation sometimes that a woman's primary responsibility is not that of an earner but of a caregiver at home. This expectation may emanate from parents or family. In emerging markets, where reliable support and baby-care centres are not found easily, it invariably leads to women compromising or redefining their careers to suit the family expectations. As stated above, in spite of the increasing literacy rates for women, a lot of professional women are found at home sometimes by choice or otherwise. Some of this is driven by these social norms.

2. Mobility: There are women who manage to successfully manoeuvre the marriage crossroads and continue working. But in dual careers, there are times where one partner's career may lead to a change in location thereby impacting the career choices of the other partner. Mobility being critical for career development for any professional, it requires a delicate balance of the two people's career preferences and ambitions. However, most often between a husband and wife, a man and a woman, it is usually the wife/ woman who voluntarily leaves her job to move with her spouse/ partner or asks for a move linked to her partner's transfer or relocation to another city. It is very rarely the other way around even if the woman has a more fulfilling career than her partner or husband. In my experience, at times this is driven by women themselves due to social expectations and for the sake of family peace.

3. Maternity: Having a child is undoubtedly a beautiful experience for any parent. Particularly for the mother, there are feelings of happiness accompanied by some anxiety. A first-time mother usually does not know what she is headed for in spite of all the advice she gets from the experienced

women in her family. Holding the child first time in your arms instils the joy and responsibility of bringing a new life into this world. As a mother you give your child your unconditional love and want to see the child succeed in life. It is a critical juncture in any woman's life. No pre-natal class or advice can prepare one for this! This is a tough crossroad and we see maximum attrition of career women in this situation. It is here that we have witnessed much struggle, given the overwhelming emotions, sometimes lack of support at home and again due to the social norms of care-giving.

Conviction in your purpose makes this journey easier and provides a boost when one is confronted with such dilemmas. It is the intensity of the belief that propels you forward and provides the much-needed momentum.

Let's review each of these in a little more detail.

MARRIAGE

As stated earlier, my first job after completing MBA was at a top FMCG as an assistant manager HR. Great company, great practices and great learnings…and I cherished every moment of it during the time that I spent there.

However, a few months into the company, I realised that having a partner in another leading FMCG Marketing team (an ardent competitor company) was not the ideal way forward for his career or mine. Even though there were no explicit policies, I realised there were softer undercurrents about how this would work out from a personal and professional perspective. Hence, both of us decided to review our options in the employment market after a year.

We both wanted to pursue the right roles for ourselves as we were driven and ambitious individuals. I found a role with Citi and decided to move on. We then got married.

Now, jobs sorted, marriage sorted, the only issue was we both were in different locations unlike when we worked together in Mumbai ! Sandeep was transferred to Pune and I was placed in Delhi. Our chalked out plan took both us to two different cities!

Convinced that I wanted to pursue a career and not just a job, I joined the role in Citibank in October 1995. Sandeep continued his role with his organisation, based in Pune. Newly married into a Punjabi family (I come from a different cultural background), I struggled to adapt to everything around me even with my best intent. There was no husband around me to translate subtleties of a new culture and cues for appropriate actions. Sandeep, sensing my struggle, made trips every two weeks. Few weeks down the line, we were yet unsure how we would get together without one of us changing our jobs. Given I was too new in my role, I felt hesitant to ask for a transfer so early with Citi, so Sandeep decided to review his options even though he was doing extremely well in his role as a brand manager. We were both convinced that we wanted our personal life and career to go hand in hand.

During the next few weeks, he had an opportunity to present in a business review to the then Vice-Chairman of the Company. The review went extremely well and at the end, as Sandeep wrapped up, he was congratulated by the Vice-Chairman, on his performance and his recent marriage. When asked how things were at home, Sandeep spoke about the struggle he and I were going through at a personal level, staying in different cities. The Vice-Chairman understood the dilemma, and told Sandeep that hopefully both the companies could make this work. He made a call to the then CEO of my organisation (an Oxford buddy of the Chairman) and requested him to gauge if there was any possibility of getting these two individuals of two companies working together in dual career struggles.

Blissfully unaware of all this, I was in a meeting with my manager that afternoon, planning the union activities a few weeks ahead, when his phone rang. On the other side of the call was the then Head of HR for Citi India. Fortunately, there was an open role in Mumbai due to attrition as these conversations were ensued concurrently. HR head checked with my manager if it would be okay for him to consider me for this role given the personal situation I was faced with. He gave him a choice that if he was uncomfortable, I would not be moved. I must confess that my manager was extremely gracious and though it wasn't easy for him to let me go, he empathised with me which bound me to Citi for a long haul that I did not realise then!

Sandeep was transferred to Mumbai in another role with his company as well. Seven months and twenty eight days after our marriage, we finally got a chance to be together…in Mumbai. Neither Sandeep nor I had compromised on our careers or our aspirations. Destiny and timing were there to help us through our trying times. Our stars were aligned. This set the ball rolling for a longer roller-coaster journey which was yet to come! Little did I know that it would later be a question of not only straddling two states, but also eventually two continents!

My experiences tell me that you need to fully believe in yourself and your capabilities for others to believe in you. Destiny is with people who believe that things will work out rather than giving up in despair. People will help you if they feel you are worth it. When you undertake a tough journey, any self-doubt can be a potential dangerous potion that will kill your morale softly. A distilled sense of self-worth instils a strong self-confidence, which is critical for behaviour and your attitude.

Thoughts, words, feelings, emotions are what really make us; but how many times a day do we pause and think 'what am I feeling' and ask 'why'?

My career for me has not been just a source of income but a bigger sense of my identity. It gives me joy and makes me complete as much as being a daughter, a wife, and a mother does. Coming from a family with a working mother, I rarely thought there was a choice of not having to work.

MOBILITY

Having a partner is all about sharing the joys and sorrows of life together. It is about being strong in the face of adversity and rising together with the tides to move forward. Sometimes couples decide to split home and work responsibilities, traditionally, with the wife focusing more at home and the man at work. At other times, some couples decide to share both these responsibilities in equal measure. Dual careers make this ride even more interesting, more so if both individuals are equally vested in their own and each other's careers. Often our work takes us to different places, provides us with the relevant experience and exposure that is key to our professional development. A lack of diversity of experiences – be it businesses or locations, narrows down our exposure and hence the career options. The tricky bit is balancing and managing two equally driven and ambitious individuals in a relationship, their careers and aspirations. It is tough but possible if there is commitment and conviction from both people.

THINK BEFORE YOU JUMP

Most intra-location moves across roles are easier as they are not disruptive to family life. It is usually the moves across locations which dual-career couples struggle with. Often we see most women opting out of their jobs to make this move happen for their spouse, even though the woman may be doing extremely well with a great career ahead of her. In some cases women may also be performing better than their spouse; however, they make this sacrifice willingly to avoid family stress. I have had numerous counselling sessions with such women and have had some success in having them step up to balance out in a dual career and not give up.

This requires effort and willingness from them personally. It is the fire of conviction in your purpose, which keeps it going. At an organisational level it required support towards instilling that much-needed confidence for such career women to take this leap of faith. This can be achieved by showing them a career path in the future and by making them more aware of their tremendous potential.

I have seen cases of some women who decided to change their jobs frequently due to their spouse moving to another location, some took a career break or took up what came their way. In most of these instances, this may not have led to a career but kept them in a job for the sake of finances and sometimes to keep them occupied. This is where the challenges and compromises come in. When it is not a thought-through choice or a choice under duress, that's when it hurts. A recent example that I recall was of a friend who was an HR manager of a big company while her husband worked for a finance company. Due to the financial meltdown, the company shut down that division. Her husband decided to take a smaller job in Dubai and relocate. This friend of mine who was doing extremely well and was slated to move on to a bigger role in the company, decided to move to Dubai for the sake of the family. She was unhappy about this decision, however she felt compelled to help her husband in the frustrating situation he was in. Hence she went along with the circumstances. She took a smaller job there and even though both of them are working, they collectively earned lesser than what she did in India with no prospects of growth with the new companies in the near future. I always wondered, *could she have changed this*? Could she have helped her husband resurrect his career in India? Was this a function of traditional upbringing? Could she not be pragmatic but a bit more persistent? Would her husband have done the same if the situation was reversed? Could her husband approach it differently and pursued something in the current location? I don't know the answer but what I know for sure is that her company lost one of their most capable employees. She gave up on a great career without necessarily being happy where she is today! May be a little more thought from both partners over emotions may have resulted in a win-win situation for them as a family.

YOU ARE WORTH IT!

I have had junior to mid-level women working with me who have been quick to jump off the career ship as soon as their husband moved to another location. I have spent several hours mentoring women at work at this crossroads, explaining to them pros and cons, to enable the appropriate thinking and decision making for their family.

Being a mobile family can be a tough yet defining experience. It does take a lot of deliberation, determination and courage to actually take the plunge each time. I have seen many men and women let go of these opportunities for fear of taking on the unknown. In my experience this has been more prevalent with women whose partners may not be mobile at the same point rather than the other way around. This is usually done to keep domestic harmony. Given the social conditioning, women choose to let go of such opportunities and their own environment is very easy with this disposition! Men often make a career choice when faced with such dilemmas. Sometimes even when they may want to take a back seat it is not easy for men. Our society is not kind to men who may want to step back and be at home !

Lately, it is heartening to see that many more young men and women in dual careers are displaying the will and courage to step out of their comfort zone and negotiate with their personal and professional eco-system to immerse themselves in such experiences. However, mobility across borders comes it with its own challenges and biases, which have to be dealt with courageously and not with preconceived assumptions or notions.

I have seen one high potential woman who was a recent victim of this when her husband relocated to Bangalore where we do not have a big office. She had erroneously pre-empted that there will not be any real roles there for her and hence came into my office to have a conversation about resigning from the service of the firm. We had a series of discussions on her career profile, her valuable relationship and equity in the company, and the bright future she had ahead of her. Given her husband had committed the move to his organisation already, we finally decided to give her a national role based out of Bangalore for a year. This made the situation much easier for her and ensured her retention in the firm. Needless to say, she was committed, worked diligently and returned to a bigger role in the headquarters later. She is still with the firm. Hence my advice to such women has been: talk, ask…. Don't assume it will not work out. You may be worth much more than you think!

I would like to share another instance of another high-performing, seasoned woman in the team, who was very keen to add an international exposure in her repertoire. She had been clear about this for a while and also had the skill set and the profile to work in developed markets. In fact, both she and her husband were aligned and keen to make this happen. They waited for the husband to take the lead for an appropriate international opportunity. Unfortunately, this took longer than they had anticipated. Hence, both of them decided that she would take the plunge. There were a few internal opportunities that were available and interested her. She took the lead and discussed with me (her manager) about a possible move, with her husband then following her. Given her performance track record and her potential, it was fairly easy to find her a meaningful role in Hong Kong and in London. She finally opted for Hong Kong and took the plunge not knowing when her husband would be able to relocate. As fate would have it, his company too finally moved him to an open role in Hong Kong and they both collectively reached where they wanted to with the wife taking the lead and the risk. Clearly a strong belief in self, knowing what one wants provided her the needed drive to move forward.

FAMILY IS WHERE THE HEART IS

In our careers, sometimes I followed my husband and at other times he followed me. Every move was thought through in terms of how it worked for us collectively and how we both together, and later as a family, benefitted from a location change. Although, I have to confess this was easier when we did not have children. After a few years we would evaluate our careers and one of us would take a plunge to do something new and the other would follow. Maybe we were also fortunate for a while, as our respective companies were able to accommodate our aspirations which kept us going as well. Our toughest move was to relocate from London to India when the children were more grown-up and also had views on this decision. I was in a newly-promoted role when Sandeep had an offer from another company that he could not refuse. So we decided to have two homes for a while, one in London and the other in Delhi. The children moved to Delhi after sometime and then after eighteen months, once I had completed my assignment in London, I relocated back as well. This was quite tough but a decision that we took as a family. It was not ideal but we made it work in the most optimum way possible, between two cities with support from our parents, staying connected on Skype and frequent travel across the globe. The distance actually got us closer as a family, as we had to make conscious efforts to ensure that the miles between us were never too much for our emotional connections. In retrospect, I learnt about how your inner strength keeps you going when you are faced with these situations.

MATERNITY

'I've yet to be on a campus where women weren't worrying about some aspect of combining marriage, children, and a career. I've yet to find one where many men were worrying about the same thing.' – Gloria Stienem

More often than not, I have seen women agonising over striking the right balance even before they reach the juncture of marriage and motherhood. Is it necessarily that tough for women when it happens? Probably yes, especially in some Asian or emerging market cultures, where the roles of care-giver and bread-earner may be rather hard-coded in the common psyche of men and women. However, the question is, should women always carry the psychological burden of this balancing act, not allowing them to dream bigger and better? Certainly not, in my view!

I have some friends who are very talented women and gave up their careers right after pregnancy. Each of us has our own drivers in life; hence they may have made the right choice of being a homemaker. However, a few of them have sometimes reflected back with me and pondered over their decision later when their children have grown up and grown their wings! This is the point at which they felt compelled to revisit their lives, trying to comprehend what their larger purpose has been or could have been, now that their children don't need their presence as intensely anymore. They seem to experience a feeling of emptiness especially if their partner/ husband were busy at work. To reiterate, I am not for a moment implying that giving up work is not right, I think it is a personal choice. If you are happy with it and it works for you, that is absolutely fine. However, one must be reasonably sure, if that is what the larger purpose demands to be content long term.

In my worldview, there are quite a few women who take this decision in haste, while also overwhelmed with the changes in their family life due to the arrival of a baby. After seeing friends, employees and family, my experience and advice to all is that when confronted with such dilemmas and anxiety, *pause for a while*. Don't rush into what may be obvious. Talk to your organisation about what may work for you and for them. This could range from flexible working, crèche support to a few months of career break. People around you *do* want to make it work. Align your expectations at work about what you can manage and what you cannot. One of the interventions which I saw as a success in the firm was a mentor group for returning mothers. They were tremendously helpful in understanding such issues for new mothers and helped them link to people who could provide them support in the organisation and outside.

Being away from work for a long time may create some gaps professionally, even though for some, passion to work remains. Second careers, for women who take breaks, is gaining some traction but has not yet been fully embedded in markets like India. It is a very workable solution for women who wish to rejoin and learn new skills at work.

I am also a firm believer in being at peace with one's choices so long as they are happy and are not taken under duress. Challenging situations in the personal realm may push many women to be guided by others' opinions, including significant others; even though that choice, may not be necessarily what they want to do. It is all about having self-belief and confidence on how much one trusts the self than others. My experience has been that the inclusive nature of women also leads them to a consensus approach on many key decisions in life, including careers. An example of this is that during the gestation period, very often (and naturally so), most women in India are guided by their mothers or mothers-in-law about discontinuing their professional jobs. During such situations, if women choose to stay at work right after motherhood, they overwhelm themselves with even more guilt of neglecting their children as they are going against the family advice.

In this aspect, it is very tough for an organisation to win over personal relationships irrespective of any employee-friendly flexible policy or an extended, maternity policy.

My experience is that once you have chosen to stay on your career path, keeping yourself constantly on the edge does not help. The road will get tougher, but second-guessing your own decision continuously, especially after motherhood, will only keep weakening you. All our children grow up *fine*! Also, in this confused emotional state, one is then unable to enjoy any sphere of life. This experience is truly very personal and is certainly difficult to generalise. Nonetheless, do whatever you can to allow yourself a peaceful and enjoyable time, both at work and at home, post-pregnancy!

PERSONAL GROWTH LIKE NO OTHER

Early 1998, I became pregnant with my first child. At the age of 26, the news left me with some mixed feelings of joy, anxiety and confusion. As expected, my parents and in-laws were overjoyed but they also had a series of guidelines and instructions about how I should keep safe during the entire phase. For the next few months, I experienced not just physical but environmental changes as well. Even though I insisted on keeping my life normal, with regular work and travel, I felt that somehow people around me looked at me differently. I was performing the role of a Talent Acquisition and Development Manager then and encountered frequent questions like: would I be able to continue travelling despite being very *normally* pregnant? I could understand that these questions were out of concern but they left me a bit uncomfortable and unsure about my own competence to do the job.

My career was very important to me and I was very keen on understanding the road ahead before I proceeded on a maternity leave. I wanted to know what role I would come back to and organsaition view on my potential. However, often the answer or advice received from managers was to focus on motherhood first, given that I was not versed with what was ahead of me in this phase of life. I was told that the role would get sorted once I come back. Unsuccessful in landing an assured outcome, I anyway went on maternity leave. Avni, my first child, arrived on time and I felt that the whole experience was not as tough as everyone had warned me. Maybe I was prepared for the worst …I truly enjoyed those few months of leave I shared with my baby daughter, apart from not getting much sleep of course! This ease during early days of motherhood was partly because her father Sandeep, being a brand manager for diapers was probably more adept at managing babies! Secondly, and on a more serious note, I managed to get a good nanny with our parents also helping us for some time.

By the third month of the maternity leave, I was beginning to crave for my work life, even though I loved every bit of motherhood. At the end of my leave, I called up the office to finalise my return date and was gladly accepted back; however, I was slightly disappointed that the role had yet not been finalised and I was assigned to some projects. As for the company seniors, they were of the view, that they were giving me flexibility (as usually requested by other women) to manage a transition back to work. However, in my head, I thought that if I left a four-month old at home to be at work, it better be worth my time! As most new mothers will tell you, it is not easy to leave a crying baby behind when you walk out of the door. Hence, I was unwilling to let myself drift on projects. Almost every week, I would be at the desk of my manager and seniors, asking for a role by identifying potential opportunities of work. That persistence and diligence paid off and I pulled all the project pieces into making it a leadership development role for myself. This was an internally focused and a proactive intervention role, unlike what I had done in recruiting, which was external and reactive. My conviction and clarity of what I wanted made me persist till I got what I wanted!

NOT BEING BOXED INTO STEREOTYPES

I learnt many valuable lessons through this experience.

I became aware that people around me had strong pre-conditioning as to how a returning mother should be treated at work, what and how much she should do. Albeit, in my best interest, I was determined not to be constricted by the view of others. I was reminded of Virginia Woolf's bright words: 'Lock up your libraries if you like; but there is no gate, no lock, no bolt that you can set upon the freedom of my mind.'

One can only emphasise the **value of drive**: Know what you want at work so that you can garner the commitment of not just yourself but others around you, to make it happen. Keep the hunger to do something meaningful, at home or at work, alive. It will provide the energy to keep you going. The passion for what you do is important and you must *feel* it integrated within your innate identity. The wisdom of Confucius' adage: 'Choose a job you love and you will never have to work a day in your life', held me in good stead every single day of this journey. Armed with ambition and drive, do not shy away from asking for what you truly want to pursue!

YOUR EMOTIONAL AND PHYSICAL STRENGTH ARE TESTED

One had to be geared up to manage multiple priorities at home and work. No matter how much your parents or husband may help you, but if you are a young mother your child is going to need you more, especially in the early stage. Stop battling with yourself.

Stop beating yourself down for being a bad mother, a bad wife and a bad employee. You are doing the best you can and keep the positive energy with the belief and conviction in your purpose. Read. Read a lot. Watch some useless soaps if you like! I find them very helpful to unwind as I don't need to work my brain at all then. Go to the gym, run. Eat well. You need to look after yourself before you can take charge of all that is happening around you.

A STRONG SUPPORT

There is also no substitute for a **support system** at work and home. Support and understanding of family members is critical especially when a woman faces this key milestones in her life. An understanding partner who can appreciate, adjust and give an equal status to his wife's career is a key force. However, the woman needs to be clear that she values her career as well. An understanding parent during maternity is invaluable. Usually, it is difficult for a woman to trust anyone else apart from her parents to leave her child behind while she is away at work. So ladies, make friends with your mothers-in-law! Finally, I think having a great nanny goes a long way in keeping things stable at home. Like a project at work, think, plan and execute for any of these three major milestones and things do fall into place. Don't dither from your purpose if there is a momentary crisis. It tides over. There are enough working women around you, who are yet happily married with well brought-up children. Reach out to a few and learn from them.

SECOND TIME WISER?

My second maternity news came to me in December, 2002. This time, wiser, I did not experience any mixed and confused emotions like the first time;, somehow I felt this was now a normal occurrence in my life. I thought it was so normal that I mentioned it to my husband only after twelve weeks of the news, which in hindsight, was a very bad decision given the furious reaction I received!

Experienced from my first pregnancy, I carried on work as usual. By this time I was on a dual assignment with a role in India along with an international project, which required me to travel extensively across the globe. Given that things were smooth with the pregnancy in the first trimester, everything just continued as usual on track with work and travel overseas. By the fifth month it became obvious that I was *putting on weight*. So, I apprised my direct manager and his first reaction was extremely amusing! He asked me my due date, which I informed him was about four months later. He seemed very perplexed with my reply and innocently asked if the baby will be delivered in five months' time or was he missing something. I laughed and said he had missed my baby bump for a while. Even today we both laugh about that incident!

By the time I was pregnant for the second time, I had spent over eight years in the firm across three assignments. With mentors in the system, I engaged much more proactively in conversations about my next move prior to my upcoming leave. I had some clear proposals about what would interest me and requested that they be considered. I laid down clear plans about how I would carry on with the role and would cut short my leave by a month, given the work cycle on one of my preferred roles (Head of Rewards and Mobility) would need me back in January. And I *was* granted the role on return! My convictions and aspirations came together.

Just when I thought things were going smoothly, God decided to test my mettle. During my seventh month of pregnancy, I was travelling on some urgent work to Istanbul (silly decision, I know!) and on my return, started to feel uneasy on the flight.

Whilst transiting through Dubai, I was hauled up by the UAE Immigration due to the obvious baby bump peeping out of my shirt. The officer requested for a medical certificate, which, I was not carrying (just plain carelessness on my part!). Therefore, he decided that I could not board the flight to Mumbai. I was not sure why he would want a hugely-pregnant woman sitting at the airport rather than sending her home! I filled my big, bewildered eyes with a few legitimate tears and pleaded to go home. When that did not work, I argued more logically stating that I should have been stopped while flying to Turkey not when returning back! Finally, I insisted that I needed to be home for medication as I was feeling unwell and voila! That worked! I was put on the aircraft to Mumbai.

Clearly the stress of the drama at the Dubai Airport played on my health and after landing in Mumbai my blood pressure shot up. After a thorough check-up my doctor decided to keep me in the hospital till the blood pressure stabilised. However a week later, she felt some complications were creeping in and hence, it was suggested that I go in for a premature caesarean section.

Sid arrived a month earlier and was a tiny baby. As a mother, I had feelings of joy coupled with guilt. I felt maybe my dedication to work and consequent travel may have triggered his premature birth, and for a long time to come I had to work on my thought process to assuage these feelings, which was difficult indeed.

On a positive note, my second maternity experience was easier and extremely joyful but I was on a huge learning curve again given it was a boy this time. Well-trained by my first baby, initially I thought I was better prepared; however, I soon realised bringing up a little boy was a much more chaotic experience than the calmer experience I had with my daughter. He was more demanding and jumpy in a few months and consumed a lot more of my physical energy. Thankfully, his father always came to my rescue when he was in one of his playful moods. This time I was even better equipped with support for two children, that enabled me to also carry out some diverse activities during maternity leave. I picked up my old hobbies and learnt a new language adding to my skills repertoire thereby using my time really well.

Coming back to work after the second pregnancy was also much easier; I had already secured Head-of-Rewards-assignment prior to availing the maternity leave and hence commenced in that role. It was a full-on, intense assignment with multiple demands, high visibility, time sensitive work to be carried out. With a wonderful team to work with, I could pace myself on work with more hours (sometime twelve to fourteen) to fewer hours (six to eight). I was more seasoned then; I knew the stakeholders well and crafted my goals focused on deliverables while managing those relationships. This was a serious role and I was committed to deliver on it despite having two small children at home. Few things that helped me were: a great support structure at home, an understanding husband and supportive work culture.

I did have a few challenges with some stakeholders who were not sure how long I might be willing to stay in office on certain days. Believe it or not, some even had a few questions on whether I could work with numbers under the stress of maternity! However, my passion to work and the will to deliver did not let me get distracted.

My takeaways from these experiences across all three crossroads have been to keep **focus on the BIG picture.** Don't give up in the short run. Keep yourself motivated with the bigger picture: just because society (and more so in Asia), gives women the *permission* to choose between career and home, we should not succumb to the social pressure of an autocratic decision while faced with issues at home or at work. Would your husband do the same? If he would – how would you feel about that? I think it is imperative that we be respectful about such choices and continue to strive to fulfil our career aspirations if that is an important dimension of our life. Having a choice should let you bounce much higher, take bigger risks and make you less conservative.

Keeping sight of the big picture of your life and where career fits, in will help you think clearly. Refelcting back to what I stated earlier, think about what would happen after the children are all grown-up, and your husband gets busier by the day.

More importantly, these crossroads in my life made me realise that there is nothing like a superwoman. A superwoman is a myth! Having been through maternity twice over, I have realised that all mothers wish to do the best for their children. We, as a wife and mother, can drive ourselves to the edge about what we did right or did not, when it comes to home, childrens food, bath and play time, development, and education. Over thinking this as a working mother, some of these aspects can also be detrimental to you apart from the child and his/her dependence on you. Let your extended family be a part of their upbringing. Let things flow their course. Likewise, stop driving yourself hard at work as you are dealing with a big change at home in the three 'M's – Marriage, Mobility and Maternity. Be kind to yourself by prioritising tasks in various focus areas in different parts of your life and get that sorted first, rather than taking on a lot more. Gauge your capacity, your support at work and home and then shoot for success in areas that feel more doable. Be upfront on this plan with family and at work. And I would quote Margaret Mead here, 'Always remember that you are absolutely unique. Just like everyone else.'

SUMMARY

A lot has been said and written about self-discovery and self-belief that provides conviction of purpose. But how many times do we really pause to just introspect and question the 'why' of any decision we take? It is unfortunate that sometimes, for women, the three 'M's almost always come with an unquestioned decision of foregoing one's career. When faced with a tough situation, especially one rooted in stereotypes and social norms, I urge you to consider the following:

- Respect your own CONVICTION to follow your dream, DON'T GIVE UP. Remember, there are many out there who are going through what you are. What will differentiate you is your own belief. There is no poison as dangerous as self-doubt.
- Believe in your capabilities and know what you want or need. This belief has to be real and unwavering. It will get further affirmed over time as one milestone leads to another and a clear path unfolds in front of you.
- Don't COMPROMISE on the quality of your dream but OPTIMISE the way you work with people and variables around you. A sense of self-worth and commitment to your dream promises priceless fulfilment. Don't rush or shy away from taking on a responsibility because it looks tough. Pause, evaluate your situation and then decide. Sometimes, focusing on the next big thing itself brings together the courage to do it all.
- There are no SUPERWOMEN, so don't strive to be one !. Take a step at a time. Know what *you* want to achieve ultimately, identify your priorities and execute step by step while keeping the belief intact. Everyone goes through their share of challenges and they *do* pass. Let the experience of your marriage, mobility and maternity not weaken your identity but rather add a defining merit to your personality.

3 CHOICES

our life's longing of who we are

CHOICES

'Destiny is no matter of chance. It is a matter of choice. It is not a thing to be waited for, it is a thing to be achieved'
– William Jennings Bryan

I have a lot of respect for people who know exactly what they are looking for and have the courage and conviction to pursue it. I admire all professionals and non-professionals, and parents who so willingly and happily give up their career to pursue what they love most, whether it be looking after their family or bringing up their children. I have friends who loved their work, but after a certain point in life, their children and family took precedence. Hence they prioritised to give more of their time and attention to family and parenthood.

When we make a choice; there is joy of having chosen something and also the anxiety of giving up something or letting it go. I truly admire such decisions, maybe because I could not take such a path and have experienced the emotion of being somewhat torn between home and work at some points in my life. Yet I convinced myself that I could manage both career and home and continued on my sojourn. Not that I perfected either but that is what I wanted for myself and was passionate about. That is the choice I made and have lived with it happily…well, sometimes stressed !

In my experience and interactions, there are many mothers who are at peace with the decision of being a stay-at-home mother and have thought it through carefully. Career breaks are not always an easy decision but there are clear motivators and drivers along with long-term thinking that goes into them. If it makes them happy then I am sure it keeps them going. Being a homemaker in my view is a very tough job. It is not always easy to manage home seamlessly for the family with utmost care. In such aspects, working mothers get away with some concessions. Sometimes I hear people wondering what stay-at-home women do all day! Having seen a few of my close friends, I know it is a hard job of managing household chores, schools and family members, especially when it is not always fully acknowledged or recognised! They truly deserve a recognition which can never be summed up by insurmountable Mother's-Day cards and flowers. They are at home because they want their family members to have a smoother life and it demands a deserving gratitude. Just because they like doing this, it should not be taken for granted. This choice should be respected.

Then there are some mothers like me who have attempted to straddle two distinct worlds of family and work. It is a stretch, but again, it is the clarity and conviction that keeps one going.

The third category is of women colleagues who are torn between choices. This can be fairly overwhelming for them. Often I have witnessed that in confronting family situations of care giving, their thinking gets clouded, which often leads to high-strung emotions. These emotions can be very strong and invoke a huge sense of guilt that may be tough to fight. More often, torn between a choice of family responsibilities and dream careers, a lot of such women that I have interacted with, choose family under duress rather than choice. Sometimes it is driven by lack of support structures while other times, by what they have witnessed with their mother during their upbringing. Some of them may feel that they actually do not even have a choice on this matter as it is expected from the family and there is no recourse. On the other hand, there are others who may feel compelled to work due to economic reasons. They need the money to be able to meet certain financial needs of the family to supplement their household income. In such cases, work becomes a means to sustain financial support rather than passion to pursue and realise one's potential. It can lead to dissonance and may not provide necessary strength that is required for prusuing a successful career. *These* are the groups that really need support to make the right choice and more importantly making peace with their choice. Both these situations can be stressful and may need support from the organisation and families.

CHANGE CAN BE INTIMIDATING

A year ago, I had a team member who was doing fairly well in the organisation and then became pregnant with her first child. She was very ambitious at work and took to her pregnancy very well, looking forward to motherhood. She remained fairly certain that she *did* want to return to work after childbirth and we proactively discussed assignments and options. Nine months flew by and she delivered a beautiful baby daughter. Overjoyed, she spent all her six months of maternity leave with her baby, and as agreed, she returned to work after her leave to her previous role. In a few weeks I started to notice that she was a bit distracted. In one of our weekly meetings when we discussed her transition back to work, she did confess that she was very stressed as a new mother without great support at home. She was struggling to cope up and was unable to come to terms with leaving her baby with the new nanny. Additionally, she also shared that her father was not too well, which was also taking an emotional toll on her. I asked her to take it easy. But knowing her, she wanted to deliver her hundred per cent at work and also at home. Over the next few months this pursuit, had an adverse impact on her and then came a moment of reckoning where she broke down completely. Her father succumbed to his illness and passed away. Being the eldest, a huge family burden fell on her shoulders. She felt overwhelmed and completely inadequate in coping with this trauma. She felt she was not doing anything well, which led to immense dissatisfaction in her own outlook to life. She felt she was a complete failure. The only dispensable piece of this puzzle was her work even though it was her passion. When she came to resign she was almost crumbling with this dilemma. Her confidence in her own capabilities was at its lowest ebb, even though she was one of our better performers. It was very sad and disheartening for me to see someone in this state. Having seen her work for a while, I was reasonably confident that she could pull herself out of this if given some support and time. She had felt hesitant to even ask for any support or days off, as she felt guilty about having joined work just a few months back. It was disconcerting for her to be thought of as someone who was again looking for a time-off (though much needed), leading to a poor impression about her professional image. Over a few discussions, I convinced her to take leave for four months to sort out her family affairs. Without a sorted family situation, not just women, but even men find it difficult to be productive at work. In spite of being convinced, that she may not be able to juggle the two worlds of work and home effectively, she took up my suggestion. She also understood that giving hundred per cent to both the sides is an impossible task and no woman had been able to achieve it till date. So, maybe she should stop striving for this surreal goal. After three months she *did* call. I could tell from her happier tone that she was back to her normal, jovial self and was truly looking forward to coming back. She had genuinely needed this time-off to set things in order for her mother, her brother and of course, her one-year-old daughter. She sounded positive and full of life as we had seen her prior to this difficult period. Her mother was with her now to provide her support as well. In a few weeks, she was back to work and even pushed me to give her more challenging assignments.

Every individual goes through these overwhelming moments. However, in cases like leaving a child at home or dealing with care-giving responsibilities for elders, some women tend to deal or react to it in a slightly more emotional way that tends to create more stress for them. More often, I see that women in these situations just need some empathy, understanding and a little breather to deal with the situation and any associated guilt that might come along. Just give them some space and time and you will find them back on their feet sooner than expected. In the above case, this lady simply felt guilty asking for a little more time-off, so much so that she decided to resign to get a hold on herself. But had she left, it would have been a loss for her and the company as well. We gave her some extended leave and she found her life back!

Another instance I recall was of this brave young mother, Rina*, who worked with me. After a few months, over a cup of coffee, we started talking about our children and to my dismay I figured that she had left her one-year-old daughter with her parents in a far-off city. She did this to ensure that the child got good care with her grandparents while she pursued her career. However, a constant sense of guilt was killing her gradually. She was resilient, thoughtful and forward-looking, but was struggling with this situation like any mother would. We had a long chat about her circumstances and I empathised with her, knowing well how tough this must be for her. We explored options of finding a better support for child-care. She was not as happy with the quality of nannies available in the city, expressed her discomfort about child-care facilities around her and wondered what she should be doing. As we discussed this, she realised the ideal situation would be if her parents could spend some time with her in her city of residence. She promised to explore that option. After a few weeks she came back happier as she had convinced her mother to move in with her, which would mean she could spend more time with her child. This gave her the much-needed bounce and

* name changed for protecting privacy

she emerged a happier individual even at work. I too felt relieved seeing Rina happy with her lovely smile back on her face.

However, in a few months, Rina was back in my office with a fairly nervous expression on her face. Her smile had vanished again! Hoping for the best, I probed her to understand what may have transpired. With tears in her eyes, she told me that she was expecting her second child. She expressed her dilemma about how she was unsure of managing one, leave alone two, even though she had always planned to have two children. I just smiled and congratulated her, told her it was a moment to enjoy and she should not stress so much about what was going to happen. Instead, she should proactively plan for how she would manage the coming times. However, Rina looked more anxious than I thought she was and she finally told me that she was contemplating resigning from work. I could see this individual breaking apart with all this imminent change around her. Her solution was to prioritise her family over her work. Work – which she was really good at and was core to who she was! Convinced about her potential I thought we needed to step in and help Rina, without being intrusive or imposing upon her family life. I calmed her down and requested her to review her support options, given the baby was due in a few months' time, while we reviewed the work options. She was much younger. I had a few other senior women who had been through similar dilemmas speak to her and share the story of their journey with her. This helped her understand that it wasn't a situation unique to her. Every mother has unconditional love for her child, which would take a priority over everything else. But there are other interests that can and should co-exist with some support, resilience and creativity. In Rina's case, these conversations helped. She went out and convinced both her parents to move in with her, ensuring quality care for her children. At work, we agreed to put her in a role for a product specialist rather than a client facing role, which enabled her to work from home with flexible timings, from time to time. This helped Rina cope with the situation when the second baby arrived. She successfully returned to work and soon was on to a high-performing track – soaring her way on to leadership! When at work she gave her best on the job, so much so that often *we* had to calm her down rather than worry about her taking liberties with her time.

Most working women go through a phase in life where they are faced with some tough choices. Some may not always know the right answer but may be pushed by family pressure. Many are goverened by strong emotions when it comes to these key decisions which can cloud their foresight. Hence sometimes these choices are not fully thought through and may get governed by thoughts and factors which may just allay anxiety and stress in the short term. But in the long run, these momentary turmoils may actually hurt them if their professional aspirations have been simply curtailed to buy peace. In some situations, women reconcile with this, while for others, it can lead to huge frustrations that can hinder their professional and personal outlook/ relationships. This can take a toll on how they work through family matters as well. A little bit of support from the organisations and families goes a long way for such women to bounce back.

DON'T MISUSE THE GOODWILL

For talent valued by any organisation, usually organisations have interventions to ensure that they are appropriately recognised and rewarded. There are development and retention strategies with exit barriers in place to ensure these high performing and high potential employees stay with the firm for a longer period. To get this attention, employees need to make themselves valuable by making key contributions, displaying commitment, and keeping themselves relevant to the context.

In cases of women struggling to balance work and family responsibilities, many organisations are rising up to the challenge by providing flexibility, undertaking the sensitisation journey, and re-skilling women. The expectation is of reciprocation from women employees through their commitment to themselves and to their career. This is a journey which is underway and by no means have we really reached the destination. Keeping up with the optimism, it seems that the steps are in the right direction, but issues tend to erupt sometimes when this trust and effort is not reciprocated. These situations maybe few, however, they are important to highlight as such incidents do put us a few steps behind.

Such is the case of Sylvia*, a mid-level employee, who had recently been moved to a larger assignment. Being a good performer, she was well-looked after in terms of good roles and rewards. About six months after performing a large client-facing role, she apprised her manager that she was expecting a baby, which was wonderful news. She remained engaged with her work, however due to her doctor's advice she requested flexibility to work from home for a few days every week in her last trimester. Sylvia's manager completely understood the validity of the request and granted her permission right away. Just a month before her delivery, she again requested that her privilege leave be clubbed with her six-months of maternity leave, which meant she would be out from work for approximately seven months. Again, this was approved as her seniors realised that being a first-time mother she was yet to get comfortable with motherhood and work being managed together. Happy with all the approvals, she proceeded on leave. Time went by. As agreed with Sylvia, and also given the fact that she had spent less than a year in her role prior to her maternity leave, the role was kept vacant for her return.

Finally, a month away from joining back from maternity, she contacted her manager and Human Resources, thanking them for all the support. However, to everyone's surprise, she also requested a role change! For a moment the manager felt that the request was due to her need for flexibility and sort of valid. But before he could consider the request and discuss the possible flexible work options in the same role, came another message. Sylvia intimated him that continuing would not be an option as she felt that she had been performing the same role for eighteen months. Technically, it was incorrect as she had been away for *seven* of those eighteen months. Since her role, an important one, was yet vacant and being managed by another employee in addition to his/her own job, it was agreed upon that Sylvia would return to the role while the manager is given a few months to look for an alternate role and also find another incumbent for her existing job. This was amicably agreed by all. She assured all the stakeholders of her commitment and signed up to her goals with a clear discussion on her promotion being considered at the year-end, irrespective.

Within a month or two of joining, Sylvia was promoted to the next level as had been one of her requests, before she stepped back into her current role. This was done in anticipation of performance and as a retention gesture, even though that year her manager had struggled to get the promotion through as there were pressures on expense and numbers. But so far so good!

As luck would have it, she was back in the room with her manager few weeks after the promotion and this time with her resignation letter. The manager was taken aback, having tried his best to support and retain a good performer. He truly struggled to understand what drove this decision and how it could have been averted. However, his frustration soon turned into disappointment. It seemed that Sylvia had traded the new promotion and compensation with another company for a similar role. The manager was left wondering if the system was leveraged inappropriately, despite all the considerations to support a young mother's career. With no more retention-related conversations, Sylvia was relieved of her duties immediately. However from a manager's and an organisation's perspective a lot of questions were left unanswered – did the organisation miss anything? Could the manager have done something to help her any further? Was this the right act on the employee's part? We all look for better jobs with better money but where does good stand?

The perplexed manager understood that one such incident is not reflective of a generic behaviour and he continued to be aligned to the organisation's intent towards providing support and flexibility for new mothers. However, given people in the department had witnessed the situation as well, there was a state of confusion within the team about what was permissible in such situations. Frank and candid conversations were held with the team and they were made to understand that this was an isolated case. All these efforts were also important to ensure that this incident did not impact chances for another young mother seeking support or flexibility.

We all know that past experiences do impact human behaviour in moving forward! Hence, it is important for women to manage situations as cited above, responsibly and professionally to not leave any unpleasant feelings behind. It undoes a lot of effort put in sensitising indivdiuals towards such situations. I am not implying that Sylvia should not have made the career change, but if she had been seeking the change prior to her promotion (given she resigned within a few weeks after), then somewhere she needed to manage the environment better by managing expectations. Being clearer on her preferences about where she wanted to work would have helped her manage the current company environment. My advice is that when one walks out of a firm, one should always leave that door open behind them... We always build/have a lot of equity where we have spent a few years and that is for keeps! You never know when you cross paths with them again.

I recall another incident which had a similar learning. This was while we were hiring for a sales team, which had traditionally been lower on gender diversity. It was a business development role entailing a fair amount of travel. Hence it had been difficult to find enough women prospects in the past as well. This time, with a conscious effort to improve diversity within the team, the search firms were given guidelines to help us with this agenda. The hiring would be on the basis of merit. Finally, a very qualified woman candidate, Tara*, with relevant work experience was shortlisted. Post-completion of the selection process, we extended a fairly competitive offer to ensure the candidate was on board. Tara accepted the offer and joined us after a month's notice period to her previous organisation. About two weeks later, I received a call from her rather unsettled manager. He told me that Tara, had just shared with him that she was four-months pregnant and would like to proceed on an early maternity leave soon, which would be leave for six (or more) months. Also, in her current state, she was unable to travel and she might need a change of role on her return. He was confused as the job specifications were discussed clearly with the candidate, at the time of hiring, about eight weeks back. On further probing by the HR Manager, the candidate shared that during recruitment, she was keen to get hired with the firm and *then* look at alternate roles.

From the manager's perspective, Tara was a great talent and knowing her intentions and 'no-travel' requirement (irrespective of the reasons), he might have yet taken the same decision of hiring her for the firm. He would have hired her for an alternate role that suited her and met her needs within the organisation at the onset. But now, having announced her as the new sales head to the clients, he was in a really awkward position that affected the team and the business, leave alone the need to find her an alternate role suiting her needs.

A tough scenario. But who was right? The manager or the concerned employee? Tara got the job but lost the relationship and the trust, which was now going to take longer to rebuild. She did proceed on leave and as requested by her, she was placed in another role on her return while another person moved in the Business Development/Sales role to provide clients the needed support. The firm lost business and the team had to again re-orient with the new managers. This situation needed to commence on an honest foundation for it to work for all.

Reflecting back, I'd say this was a real dilemma. It may have been prudent for Tara as well to gauge the demands of the role vis-à-vis what she was able to do before arriving at a final decision of taking up the offer. She was very competent and would have been hired for a role better suited for her needs through a fair process. With a little more thought, she would have led to stronger and a more meaningful relationship at the onset. Such issues make situations difficult as they may reinforce stereotypes even though the organisation has policies and procedures to deal with this appropriately. It is also contingent on us women to be upfront and deal with such conflicts in a way that it is a win-win!

MOVING FORWARD

No one situation or choice can be or should be generalised. We need to be respectful of each individual's choices as everyone has his or her own priorities, be it at home or at work, or elsewhere. At work, I do see a rising amount of awareness and an effort on part of various organisations to focus on support systems for women. Flexibility, maternity policies over and above the statutory requirements, crèches/ child care support and so on… are taking root in the industry and it will take a few more years for this to spread more widely. This journey is relatively new and yet underway, though I think we are headed in the right direction. For the right talent who contribute and add value, I see a growing number of organisations willing to bend backwards to retain them and work around their needs to manage work and family. Like for any other employee, if women want to seriously pursue their careers, then it is contingent on them to be committed and tenacious when faced with multiple demands. It is not always easy; however, it is neither easy for our male colleagues and they may have different challenges. My only request to all is to not give up without trying!

SUMMARY

Our choices reflect the kind of person we are. Ultimately it is not about being right or wrong but what *you* want and what gives you a sense of fulfilment and achievement, driven completely by *your* priorities. Many women, especially when they embark on their three 'M's – Marriage, Mobility, and Maternity, get caught on the horns of a dilemma. This takes a bigger toll on them rather than the attempt of executing their choice would. Without the fear of failure, just evaluate what you treasure more and take the plunge. But keeping in mind the following steps might help you along the way:

- Being a mother or a professional, or both, is an individual's choice driven completely by respective circumstances. Nothing is better than the other. It all depends on what makes you happy, Choose for yourself and give it your best.

    Once decided to manage work and family, be open to seek help in making your choice a success. You may be surprised to see how organisations, managers, or even your own support system will be there to assist you in the attempt to make it happen – you have to take the decision and drive it first.

- Finally, foster a trusting relationship with your employer. Remain clear in your conscience and respect all the help that others extend. Go through your pursuit with authenticity and focus. Appreciate the efforts that others around you make to ensure it all works for you both personally and professionally....because, that also reflects a choice and the kind of person you get viewed and treated as.

4 COURAGE

to explore the road less travelled

COURAGE

'Success is not final, failure is not fatal: it is the courage to continue that counts' – Winston Churchill

DEMANDS OF THE NEW WORLD

Corporate Jungle – Survival of the Fittest or Survival of the Savviest?

In some ways, the corporate world still remains a jungle. One encounters all kinds of people: pack leaders, followers, some who stick to their set roles and patterns, and others who are willing to test the boundaries to take on predators. The management capabilities continue to evolve in a constantly changing environment leading to an increasing demand for more intense engagement at work. We are required to be agile, responsive, adaptive, and flex our styles to the multiple challenges thrown at us. All this puts a lot of stress on our softer skills. How quickly we imbibe this versatility, becomes critical to thriving in the long run. Competition at work often leads to politics. Politics may lead to setting agenda and one can be easily victimised by this process. As the pyramid narrows and race to leadership gets tougher, your competitors may look for the slightest pretext to pull you down, including your gender, the way you manage or behave.

Climbing the corporate ladder is equally tough for men and women. There is less space at the top, competition is rife, and technical capabilities are abundant. Hence, more often than not the softer people-skills become the differentiator in this competitive environment. I have been fortunate enough to work with some very inspirational and driven individuals who understood this early in their career and imbibed these softer skills adeptly and timely, that was necessary for their growth and managing transition. Their learning was on an ever-rising continuum. It was their ability to be visionaries that helped achieve great results. As they undertook this journey, I saw that it took a lot of courage and inner strength to continue the climb because as it got steeper, the risk was higher and the path ahead, unclear. Many a shark was waiting for them to fall in the sea of darkness beneath.

In a post, published by Dan Goleman, Ph.D. on Apr 29, 2011 in The Brain and Emotional Intelligence – Are Women More Emotionally Intelligent Than Men?', he states that, 'There are many tests of emotional intelligence, and most seem to show that women tend to have an edge over men when it comes to these "soft" skills for a happy and successful life. That edge may matter more than ever at the workplace, as more companies are starting to recognise the advantages of high EI when it comes to positions like sales, teams and leadership.'

If you review the above demand for softer skills, I find that women are usually better placed as they are brought up to always be more adaptable to changes. It is all about how we define the purpose, plan the path and focus on work that is aligned to peoples' needs rather than just business targets.

Be it demands at work, competition with peers, or leveraging technical or people skills, it is driven by the belief in one's dreams and having the passion to fulfil them. Coupled with some skills or higher EQ that women may have more of, or a different perspective they may add in the board room, the impact of this is finally contingent on their courage to pursue this chosen path. Courage may have different facets encompassing taking charge, taking conflicts headlong, taking risks, stepping up your game, pushing the boundaries against all odds! The consistent pattern among all facets is a reinforcement of your beliefs that creates the magic to keep going on. I too have had my ups and downs but the courage of my convictions did not let me down. Lets review these facets…

TAKING CHARGE

At a basic level, we work for a living and our companies reward us for our contributions. However, most of us also derive a larger self-identity from our work. Whether right or wrong, it becomes an integral part of our lives. Some indivudals may be unsure and coast along, in such cases life takes over and gives you a plan, especially if you have none. We call it our destiny and may sometimes relinquish control of things that can be detrimental of our identity. It takes a significant amount of courage to actually make conscious choices along each step, do everything that it takes to honour those and shape who we are.

I am agnostic about how and to what degree various individuals prefer to do this. However, for me, taking charge of self has been a clear driver in the way I have gone about my career. Through my various assignments in India or overseas, most choices of roles, locations, managers or teams were solely *my* choices. Whether to work through a tough family phase or to move into a new assignment, it was always a thought out decision. Of course, it needs to align with the needs of the organisation and grounded in your reality, but nobody knows you better than yourself! You need to have the strength to back yourself, before the organisation can have the courage to stand behind you. This belief in self has instilled a sense of responsibility and self-reliance in me. Sometimes I got it right and sometimes I did not. But there have been no regrets. Instead, my learning cart has overflowed with a bounty of experiences which I will treasure forever. My mantra has been to not depend on things to take shape by destiny. Success comes to those who work for it. We must keep reassessing and align if need be, but never lose sight!

DEALING WITH ISSUES HEAD-ON

Very early in my career, I realised that dealing with issues head-on is important. While our work speaks for itself, in times of conflicts choosing to take a back-seat and being silent is not an option.

I have come across both men and women who have been apprehensive about working with a woman manager. In my various roles, I sensed that there were prevailing mis-perceptions about how women managers were not always pragmatic or tough in their decision making….whilst others felt they were control freaks … at other times, a few groups thought women managers were emotional and not objective. Was this driven by deep seated biases or was this real?

In one instance, one of my close associates, Reema* had a male subordinate who, in his limited view and interactions, decided that she was no good! This probably was driven by what values he grew up with and his views about a woman's capabilities in general. As a result, he would constantly skip her and go for all key decisions or activities to her manager, who had a similar mindset and connected with him. Reema felt sandwiched between these two layers and it started impacting her relationship with other team members who were beginning to lose respect for her and were talking and watching this interaction. Reema's role was gradually becoming ineffective and her ability to cater to her clients was getting impacted adversely. She felt neglected and humiliated. She tried to be amicable at first and engaged in constructive discussion without much headway. However, in spite of her repeated discussions and inclusive style, the colleague's behaviour did not improve. Possibly, Reema's inclusive style was seen as a sign of weakness, aggravated by her manager's lack of efforts to correct/advise the colleague of appropriate behaviour.

Reema was truly stressed. As the situation got worse, she reflected upon the situation and decided that it was time to take charge and garner support. So she reached out to a seasoned professional she knew, in one of the other teams and explained the situation to him constructively. He heard her objectively, empathised with the issues and advised her to take the appropriate firm action that an effective manager should do in such a case. Reema needed someone to push her on this path. Unlike her usual *modus operandi* of reaching out, discussing and getting to an agreement, she decided to flex her style and confront her team member on his conduct in a straightforward way. But he did not take Reema seriously and tried to justify his behaviour without being open to understanding the feedback. He insisted that his actions were based on departmental practices and he was leveraging her manager as a mentor and not intentionally skipping her. This was not entirely correct as many times he would execute work priorities without keeping Reema in the loop. Hence a formal performance discussion ensued with a polite, but direct admonition for his behaviour. Concurrently, Reema also had a polite yet firm discussion with her manager and requested him to let her deal with the situation in her way. She had to explain to her manager that a 'not-so-happy team issue' at hand also reflects poorly on him as a leader and he should let her manage it. He backed off and gave her the space to manoeuvre.

The employee was not happy with the confrontation but understood the seriousness of Reema's tone and demeanour. Over a period of time, the relationship changed from negative to neutral and they continued to work together for a year till he moved to another role. Reema stood her own in the right way and earned the credibility of her leadership style with her team. She drew a line on what she thought was inappropriate and defined what liberties were permitted with her as a manager. That set the tone right!

As women, we often get constrained by our need to be inclusive and avoid being confrontational. It is important to make an objective read of the situation and take on issues appropriately but directly. I have learnt that the courage to deal with such issues only grows from one experience to the next! **Conflict management** is part of growing up and so long as you have the right intent, coupled with the courage to take the situation head-on, you will find a resolution. It creates some discomfort initially but your conviction will provide you the courage to deal with it.

TAKE SOME RISKS

We all wish to grow meaningfully in our professional careers. However, the definition of growth may vary from one individual to another. For some people, growth comes from changing jobs, new experiences, and for some it means changing geography. For others it may mean moving up the corporate ladder.

So, *what is growth*? It is essentially an enhancement in responsibilities, be it revenues, team size, products, span of control and so on. I believe growth is not just about chasing titles or levels blindly. Many times, I have witnessed that people chase their next level, designation or grade as defined in the company ladder. Is this real growth or an elevation of status ? Having observed practices across the workplace, I think the distinction between of levels in the ladder/ designation and real responsibilities is important and critical to understand. A real role will provide the appropriate exposure, experience and education important to propel a career forward whereas a change in level or deignation may get some monetary benefit but no learning. Change in roles implies taking risks and bets on yourself as it can put you out of your comfort zone.

I think it is very important to be clear about what growth means for *you*. Have the courage to **stand out** with your learnings! Have the courage to take a few **risks** and do different things at work!

I have taken some risks with different roles and geographies, which were a part of my growth and continuous learning. I made mistakes, I learnt, and I grew. Some risks work out and some may not, but there is learning in negative experiences as well. Whoever achieved greatness by playing it safe! This philosophy will keep you going, more so in the moment when you question your decision to stay on at work. As J.K. Rowling has beautifully summed up, 'It is impossible to live without failing at something, unless you live so cautiously that you might as well not have lived at all, in which case you have failed by default.'

Whilst I was working in one of my regional roles earlier in my career, one of the seniors requested me to work on a critical HR technology project that had a lot of investment riding on it. This was in the year 2000. I truly had no real insights into technology then and had not been engaged with a development project like this one… I was simply a regular user of emails and internet! However intuitively, it seemed exciting and I decided to explore it. Am so glad I did this…. It was an experience wherein I chartered unknown territories, acquired some key, futuristic skill sets of understanding the nuts and bolts of technology. It was hard work, time consuming….I stumbled a few times, made mistakes, but did learn a lot. The risk and rewards paid off not just for the project I undertook, but the experience also played a critical role in my future assignments, making me much more tech savvy.

It may not always be easy to navigate between taking risks and taking charge, especially for women given how they are socialised. Some of this may not come naturally at work …. Trust yourselves, reach out to people, trust your mentors, let go off your inhibitions and perceptions of the past. To move ahead on an unchartered territory and taking a few bets is the key to building your experience, especially for leadership roles. Early bets in life will also help you measure your options of opportunities and provide you with skills. Am grateful that this has worked for me. I too have had failures, projects gone wrong, strategy not executed well. In such circumstances, keeping oneself honest, reviewing gaps and improvising helped. I have had to let go of my negative energy while taking these chances and have had to ensure that I move ahead with the positive outlook and a clear vision of what I wanted. That helped me focus on my efforts, strategies and plans towards achieving the goal. This also ensures no scope for self-doubt.

COURAGE TO STEP UP WILL HELP YOU THINK LONG-TERM

To keep ourselves relevant in the long run, it is imperative to focus on the quliaty of the role. A common theme I have observed is that most women focus on the long-term interest of their family, their teams, colleagues and friends. However, they seem to forget about their own interests when it comes to their long-term career. Social upbringing helps us focus on the larger family picture around us, but does not encourage us to think about ourselves "*selfishly*". The reason I say this is, if women are serious about career and safeguard their own interests at work and at home, a lot gets taken care of for the surrounding environment and the people who matter to us as they are fulfilled more holistically. At work, I often find professional women struggle in resolving issues of work-home balance. Hence any job that helps one to manoeuvre efficiently between the two in that moment becomes a preferred option. I am not implying that this strategy is inappropriate as these choices are personal. All I am trying to highlight is the long-term impact of this, if women aspire for a leadership role later.

A courageous mindset is the key to keep pushing along, against odds. Try to be creative with your work schedules and approach. I have seen successful women leaders go through some short-term hardships, which were tough but not impassable. In case of care-giving, they often tend to make a work-support system with extended family, friends and husband share the role of the care-giver as they simultaneously stretch their professional goals and take up work challenges. Many a time when I went through tough times at home with children being unwell or something similar, I would work from home or have one of my family members be with us, depending on the situation. Sometimes, in the short term, a project would suffer but I would compensate for it by working harder and smarter the next week. Often, you can push the system to measure you on output and not necessarily on how and where it was done. But in this situation, if a woman was to deny herself the project or the role that is a bit demanding, she will be denying herself growth. The reality is that children fall ill, parents do become unwell, and your husband will be busy with work, but if your work is also one of your focus areas as well, push yourself to find the right support system at home. And remember, this problem is not unique to you; we all face this in our lives. You have to be emotionally determined, physically strong and creative enough to manage these issues. It takes courage to keep pursuing your dream, while making the canvas of your dreams wider and wider.

In my experience, the more you focus on stepping up for your aspirations, it becomes clearer for you to steer yourself through your current role as well. Often the work objectives and your efforts start yielding success, positioning you for your next role. To me, this has been a critical component of how I planned my career. A slightly mid-to-long term perspective helped me tide over the short-term problems at home or at work, kept me focused on the skills and experience I needed for the future, and kept me going to make connections, watch the environment and flex myself towards the objective I was focused on.

This mindset has helped me anticipate and manage competition for a growth opportunity or a promotion and egged on my energy to keep going. I took an assignment in New York to gain exposure for my next few roles. In this role, I learnt about the various global processes, personalities and peculiarities. While I experienced all the global nuances of working in the headquarters, I also planned a move back to an Indian assignment in the HR advisor space, within twelve months. My global exposure in New York and Singapore ensured that I got a strong consideration for the role back home as "Global" India was starting to emerge. When the role opened up in India, I applied, was interviewed for it, and secured it on the basis of my relevant prior experience.

As women, we should not underestimate ourselves or step away from challenges when faced with dilemmas. Whether it is about negotiating challenging assignments, taking on mobility, or gaining exposure at work that pushes the boundaries, it is all up to us.

UNCONCIOUS BIASES....TESTING THE BOUNDARIES... QUITE LITERALLY!

You grow up being taught that God created us as equals. However, it sometimes seems that it is we who set the boundaries by defining the norms, practices, etiquette and style for each gender. During my professional journey, there have been a few times where my patience, learning, flexibility and dignity were put to test. However, my inner beliefs kept me going, be it during job transitions, pregnancies or geographical changes. Human nature is subtle and very often we are unaware of the drivers of our own behaviour. Deep-seated beliefs, experiences and perceptions shape our world-view and how we interact with people, communities and gender. At work, these become very acute and influence our mind, resulting in relationships that sometimes are difficult to fathom.

In my experience there can be and needs to be more sensitivity to how people, especially women, work across cultures. Differences in perspective, styles or actions can be honed very constructively creating a win-win for all. However, at times these differences may be misunderstood and judgment applied to 'what's being said' without really deciphering the real motive behind actions. Different meanings get attributed to actions contrary to what may be communicated. Behaviour gets interpreted in divergent ways to what one's intent might be. It saddens me that we lose so much talent and productivity, due to these biases that some people carry across the world. These biases are shaped from individual experiences and sometimes even ignorance and can drive how people interact with various gender or cultures at workplace.

Women continue to face this dilemma as society across has defined its expectations from men and women over time. Traditionally, men are the bread-earners and women are the care-givers but it is never that straightforward. This has always confused me...as I have seen numerous women around me suppress their professional aspirations to let their partners flourish. This may not even be the best strategy for a relationship to work well. Also, very often I find women taking a short-term view of their work, rather than a long term view about their career. This makes it really tough for women who *do* want to pursue careers seriously as it reinforces the stereotype. As I mentioned earlier many returning mothers are often faced with a foregone conclusion on flexibility or a preference for fewer responsibilities that do not add to career growth. This *does* frustrate a lot of serious, career-oriented women, who finally leave, faced with a Hobson's choice.

Unconscious bias reflects even in the style of management that women are expected to exhibit. Given the innate nurturing quality that women are expected to possess, expectations at work, too, get governed by the same. I realised through some harsh experiences of my own, that a woman is expected to have a quiet, personable, care-giving demeanour. If women are too assertive at work, colleagues may view her negatively and call her "aggressive". If one displays ambition too overtly, one is termed as too "self-centred and selfish". If one speaks up and has a viewpoint in management teams, one is considered "abrasive". All these attributes are perceived positively for men and are considered as drivers of their success but they are derailers for women. There is pervasive competition at the work place, so these preconceived notions about women prevail in the minds of both men and women.

Over the years, even though I did not engage in much office gossip, little did I realise that it did not necessarily absolve me from pointy fingers! As I transitioned to senior roles, I had to be sensitive to this and tweak my behaviour while being authentic to the extent that it did impact my work. It was very tough managing a few work groups, but it was important to be engaged and persistent to ensure that people understood my purpose and intent. I learnt to change a few minds. My mentors and buddies always gave me a lot of strength and support. There were finally a few I could not convert because of their own strong belief of how a woman should or should not behave and any non-conformity to that would qualify me as a bit *deviant*. You can't win the entire world!

On cultural sensitivity, I realised that Asian work ethics are driven by our sociological factors. Most middle-class families in India put a premium on education, considering it to be an elixir for the next generation to do better than the last one. Competition is extremely tough in emerging markets and it is about the survival of the fittest. There is no social secuirty so no job means no support for even basic livelihood. Hence to secure a good career and financial stability, academic excellence is at the forefront. There is a push to to get ahead in the race at any cost even in schools. This can result in an imabalance between competition and collaboration and can also lead to less sensitivity to social or softer dynamics at play.

Work is not a *part* of people's life in emerging markets, it *is* their life. A lot of emotional and physical energy gets vested in it. Boundaries between professional and personal lives are very blurred or even non-existent. The concept of time is fluid.

The struggles in an emerging market upbringing provide the much-needed drive, hunger and ambition, but not always the necessary tools to develop leadership capabilities to succeed globally. Social skills are not taught or given importance to in the academia. This is a very critical success factor on how people adpat at work, when they are working in a more flourishing developed markets culture. This finesse is picked up on the job. Scarcity of liberal mindsets is prevalent. Hence successful leaders understand the criticality of these skills and mould themselves to various cultures. However, the journey takes a while. Now super-impose this cultural bias on gender in a cross-border environment!

In the light of our desire to test new waters, Sandeep and I relocated to London. Citi, being an organisation that values mobility, provided me with an exciting opportunity in Europe. In spite of being with the same organisation, it turned out to be a remarkably different experience. My colleagues were very welcoming and a whole new world and exciting challenges awaited me.

As I commenced my assignment in Europe, simple adaptations had to be made to the way of communication, dress code, and food (that I loved), which were all notably, very constructive interventions for me to fit in with the larger group. The harder part was work codes which I would like to elaborate on as it was my biggest learning that made me grow further as a professional.

I recall, my first few months in the new office were quite exciting, but also a bit unsettling as it was all so new to me. A large part of the team that I worked with were long-term residents or nationals, and clearly were used to a certain *type* of behaviour or *culture* that probably *was* different than other places that I had worked in (Asia and North America). A few people were very forthcoming and extended their support whilst dealing with a few others sometimes made me feel uncomfortable as I was unable to fathom them. No matter how hard I tried, somehow I struggled to open the door to the gates of friendship. They were reclusive, not that anyone said anything discomforting. However, the cues of non-verbal language were confusing and isolating at times.

Coming from an Asian background and that too from an emerging market, I focused on work as an extension of my personal life, connectivity playing an important role. The style of communication was probably a little more direct for the workplace. I understood later that these attributes were not culturally aligned. During my initial days at the European office I stumbled, said polictially incorrect things but worked really hard to adpat! At times, I could not understand why people would perceive me differently. Was it simply because I was too focused on getting work done? Did I really need to engage in discussions even though some of them were not really interested in talking to me? There was nobody to explain. Regardless of my best intentions and focus to contribute and add value, sometimes I felt something missing. A few times I fell prey to the departmental politics more so because I did not belong to a clique. At other times, I was shot down because I was working for a senior manager who some team members might not have been too fond of, but due to his seniority he could not really be impacted. I had to garner all my positivity and courage to deal with this transition.

Reflecting back, I understand better the subtlety of communciation and politics in some developed countries, which one was not used to earlier. I had to learn to read the tea leaves albeit it was a slow process for me. Sometimes the silent campaigns in office took the better of the team. It was a dynamic that consumed other talented people, who could not read between the lines. But it was imperative to manage this to be successful and I had to learn it to the best of my abilities. Each geography works differently and am sure someone from a developed market who is transitioning into an emerging market like India may experience similar challenges in the reverse way! The key is to adapt, understand and mould your style.

Gradually, I learnt that communicating and understanding messages in Europe was not always about what is said (as in Asia) but a lot that is unsaid. One had to understand the subtexts, which was not as easy for me to do in the early days. I increasingly focused on consensus building and toned down my bias for action. Engagement was key and had to be initiated. Reading subtle cues was a key attribute for me to imbibe. I learnt the hard way that having a direct communication style in such a culture maybe considered rude as much as being indirect in Asia is considered insolent. Being emotional and driven openly especially at work is perceived to be overwhelming unlike in Asia where being passionate is a sign of commitment and engagement. Many such dilemmas surfaced. I had to work on myself to fit in better with the work environment. As I learnt new ways of working through observation, work groups and peer mentoring, I continued to do what I did well, which was manifest my passion for my work. Very rarely, would any such issues distract me from the deliverables. But placing myself in a new culture was undeniably tough yet equipped me with a different and important perspective!

I remember, once whilst I worked overseas, there was a colleague of a different nationality who had been giving me a tough time by being passively aggressive. This person carried a somewhat difficult attitude towards me for reasons not quite evident to me. It felt that this person was constantly looking for an opportunity to nail me down. One day, clearly quite upset with what my team had done on a project, this person barged into my office without my permission, threw the door open and started screaming audaciously at the top of their voice, accusing me of incompetence, implicating I was incapable of getting anything sorted. In a rude and loud tone, this person outlined the impact of this mistake on the business. After a minute, the person's voice was deafening and the entire floor became aware of the ruckus going on in my office. There was sudden silence outside my office, on a floor with a hundred people. I was not sure I heard all that this person was shouting about, but noticed the aggressive body language and decided to exercise my calm by requesting the person to sit down and have a peaceful discussion. Clearly that was not on the cards. That day my emotions overwhelmed me and I could have shouted louder than this individual, but my tolerant roots held me back and I simply asked the person to leave in a firm tone. The individual stomped out with the same vigour that they had come in with. The floor was quiet; my team members walked in to check if I was fine. I nodded in affirmation even though my eyes were swelling up. I was not sure what happened and *why*.

Getting a hold of myself, I called our manager and narrated the incident. Then there was only one question I wanted him to answer, which was, that if I had behaved like this with this person, what did he think would have happened? Who permitted this person to behave like this? My manager was honest enough to tell me that he had a real problem with this kind of behaviour and will address it on priority. I put the phone down. After four hours, my manager having had the right conversations and taken firm actions, this person was back in my room profusely apologising for the inappropriate behaviour. The fact that the organisation had taken the right recourse really made me feel reassured but the person's apology had no meaning for me. Because what I had seen that day was a larger issue. A person was reacting to me without knowing me at all, had no knowledge of my background, no working relationship. What could have kindled the audacity to behave in this way? Who allowed this person to take this liberty? Maybe because I was different? Spoke differently? Or the person simply did not like the way I was?

Some of these questions go unanswered. But I am very grateful to the organisation for having taken the appropriate recourse with the individual for such inappropriate behaviour. However, the insult and the hurt to my emotions were inexplicable. Nevertheless, gathering courage, I did not let this ever impact my self-esteem attributing this to the individual's own issues. I actually felt sorry for this person, for their insecurities and lack of sensitivity that would hinder the individual's success. Preserving your self-esteem is really in your control. When you are faced with such a circumstance, it is very important to draw a line as we operate in a zero-tolerance environment with regards to respect at work. I do not behave inappropriately with anyone and I will not let anyone treat me inappropriately.

It took tremendous courage to hold myself back and display a dignified reaction, yet taking a stand on unacceptable behaviour. However, my reactions stood me in good stead in the future and I was perceived to be a better leader, more importantly, a better human being.

'You may not control all the events that happen to you, but you can decide not to be reduced by them.' – Maya Angelou

SELF-BELIEF TESTED AGAIN...NEEDED ANOTHER PUSH AGAIN TO TAKE A RISK

In London, someone I had worked with earlier, tapped me to apply for the role of Head of Human Resources for Commercial Bank. I was not that keen on this role, as it was a lateral move and the slate of candidates was a strong one with two candidates from the UK team with local experience. I was unsure about this change as I was well-settled in my current position. I was working for a Regional Function Head with some good work to do. This new role would entail working with a direct of a regional head (so a step down on the level of reporting) even though it was a client-facing role. That was the only positive drive for me, as I liked the commercial side to HR. Yet, I was unsure whether it was worth it, but looking back I could not have been more wrong about that! It was probably one of the best moves I'd made. However at that time, the hiring manager had to really convince me to move in the right direction, by showing me the potential future growth and probably one day even getting a shot at the larger HR Head for Corporate and Investment Bank. Either I underestimated myself or felt I was not ready for the risk, without a guarantee for the future, only to have realised now that there are no guarantees in life for anything! After much coaxing, I agreed to take up that role. Within twelve months, my hiring manager left (he may have planned this!) and the financial crisis set in. I happened to be in the right place at the right time and got promoted to the larger role of heading HR for Corporate and Investment Bank within a year. I was young and felt really enthused to find myself where I was then and was raring to go.

However, the question is, had he not pushed me, would I have taken the bet? Maybe not, and then, where would I be now?

From then on, I realised that I needed to push myself a little more on taking risks planning for the next move and not get pushed out due to any biases.

A WOMAN'S DOMAIN?

We often encounter sectors, professions, roles that are traditionally not considered to be a woman's domain. Some examples of these are technical, manufacturing, client facing and sales roles where less women are seen at middle to senior levels,. While some women may choose not to tread on these paths, those who demonstrate the courage to do so often outshine their male competitors, in my experience ! Some planning and preparation always helps.

When I took on the role of the Corporate and Investment Bank HR Head, it was quite a stretch from the experience I had by then. Some of the things that I did were:
- Diligence on the role and what was really required: both informally and formally
- Engaged with stakeholders to understand their view on internal and external environment
- Discussed with the hiring manager and stakeholder how I could contribute to the role.

This helped especially when one was taking on a larger new role and built a greater stakeholder confidence and buy in.

Moving on to the Head of HR for Corporate and Investment banking was the best learning experience I ever had. The first few times I met the business teams for the role, I suspect that some seniors probably did not even notice me. They seemed to have an fortress around them where there was no space for anyone unless one was a part of the *club*. There is no short cut to success. They tested my mettle at work, through stressful business situations, gauged my judgement and validated my HR advice to get the needed comfort if I was worth their time and attention. My understanding of their business was quizzed continuously in my early days in this role. I had to prove myself to earn respect from the bankers! They gauged my tenacity through my hard work and energy. It was apparent to me that I had to understand their business at least as well as them to earn my seat on the table and get the respect for the role I was designated for.

I recall after a few months I was finally considered *worthy* and was invited for my first management meeting. I got inducted with much warmth with many members of the senior leadership banking team present. When I started to introduce myself, what struck me was that around the table it was a group of white males in their mid-forties or above. Post a formal introduction, I smiled politely and said, 'Gentlemen, I think I add colour from every perspective here, be it my gender, colour of my skin, the way I talk and also, I don't always wear black or grey! So, this will be one hell of a ride.' I guess that did break the ice and everybody had a good laugh about it. That was a great start to a wonderful and an everlasting friendship.

So I was inducted into the camp only after I had earned my stripes through intense engaement and diligence. What struck me the most was that once I was in the camp, gender did not matter at all; I was just one of them. Maybe the direct style of communication and identifying myself that intensely with work, clicked better in this environment. The bankers never differentiated who I was, where I came from, so long as our purpose and goals were aligned at work t worked well for me for five years that I was in this role. Probably it was this element of the relationship of equals that made it a great partnership !. I learnt immensely from this assignment and have a lot of regard for the business irrespective of what we went through later in a financial crisis. It is an experience that remains ever so dear to me as I felt I could value add and contribute as in integral member of the team. I am grateful to them for making me realise my potential!

This business too stood by me through good and bad times, which bound me to them with sincerity. Even though my own journey was smooth, I did witness that we needed to focus on improving gender diversity especially at the leadership levels. We had women attriting from the work force at junior to middle levels due to extensive travel or work pressure from clients. The ones who *did* make it to leadership roles or operated in senior roles seem to have made significant changes to their lifestyle at home or work but had to toughen themselves for the challenge first.

As I reflect back, this was not always related to the organisation, it was also to do with a larger environment of an industry where roles require extensive travel and staying away from home for a period of time, for both men and women. Further, some seasoned and capable women were not always vocal about their aspirations which made it difficult to review and position them for bigger roles or significant deals in the market. Some of them seemed to be happy with what was given to them rather than asking for what they really wanted to work on. One can always try and change the world, but that may take a while and I wondered if some of these women needed to push a little more.

Client facing or sales businesses are quite demanding on time and effort and can sometimes be tough for women to balance with other priorities. However we need more women there to change the culture, making it more inclusive of different styles. I have worked with business heads who wished to have a more diverse management team but a lack of women pipeline at one or two levels below hindered this. So the question is, where are the women? Is there a pipeline? In a high paced client working environment, many women back out much earlier in their careers. This happens mainly due to work timings of coming in early at the break of dawn, which surely doesn't work for young mothers. Also, the working culture sometimes needs to be more comforting for women. Having been through this myself, and having worked with a lot of such people, I believe they want to make it work but need some sensitisation and organisational strategies to make it work for women. A lot of them may have never worked with senior women and probably don't know how to, so it is contingent on the organisation and the women community to get these collegaues up the curve. In the business that I worked with, we changed the timings at work for certain units, introduced job shares and had a few seniors "sponsor" a few emerging high potential women by championing their cause in talent meetings. They were provided with mentors (

men and women) who could help them adpat to the demands of the environment. It helped us curb attrition at middle to senior levels which we hope over a few years would translate into a more diverse leadership team.

My advice to women is that don't back off, and *please* don't leave! We need many more women out there to show the courage to stay on, making this easier for the next generation of women to strive and thrive.

AGAINST ALL ODDS – LET YOUR FAITH BE LARGER THAN YOUR FEARS

When you find your passion in work, it does not remain work anymore. However, there are cycles of good and tough patches in life. Not all of this is under our control. Life sometimes tests our courage in ways that we may never imagine – requiring us to pull up every ounce of strength, grit and determination – call it whatever you might! It takes a huge amount of belief and courage to remind yourself, who you are.

I often think that women are able to fare better in such personal or professional crises, probably owing to the fact that they are conditioned to pull together for their loved ones as well. However, it is very important for them to realise that it probably takes far much more strength to do the same for themselves. Women need to look after themselves physically and psychologically. Courage can pull you forward only when your physical health can hold strong.

In London, a sunny day in June, 2009, I returned home from work, feeling a bit feverish. I had a cold and a sore throat. Given the mercurial London weather, I was sure it was one of the seasonal flu bugs that had found me, at a very busy time of the year in office. There were some important deliverables at work and a few business meetings that were time-sensitive and had kept me fairly busy. I popped in an analgesic hoping to feel better by the morning.

But even at seven in the morning, I was not feeling as good. I got the children ready for school and spoke to my husband who was in Singapore that week. The fever still hadn't gone. As I thought of work, the adrenaline rushed in and I picked up my bag, coat, and a pack of medicines and was off to the tube station. Everything seemed hazy before me. At work, the cough worsened and my body ache became more and more acute with every passing hour. I could hardly work; hence decided to return home early. I managed a hot chicken soup telling myself that tomorrow would be a better day. I popped another tablet and went to bed, feeling very grateful to my nanny for tucking the children into bed. Next morning I felt extremely dreary and I had to call in sick and work from home. By the evening I felt worse and had to call a friend, who was a doctor, who prescribed an antibiotic. I decided to go to the clinic next morning. However my condition got even more traumatic by night with a severe backache and incessant cough. Given my husband was away, my nanny was kind enough to help with a hot-water bottle that gave me temporary relief from the backache.

By the morning, things worsened. My cough aggravated, with an overarching chest ache and I had to rush to the washbasin to throw up. As the overpowering urge to hurl took over me, I shut my eyes, emptying my lungs and my stomach. As I opened my eyes and looked down, my heart skipped a beat. The basin was splattered with blood. I knew there was something very wrong with me and it just couldn't be a case of the common flu!

My children had panicked the moment they saw me and I requested my nanny to take charge of them while I sorted myself out. I called up my friend who arrived promptly and took me to an Accident and Emergency Centre in the nearest hospital They took me in immediately and conducted a whole battery of tests from tuberculosis to blood diseases to lung issues. The final diagnosis indicated a severe bout of pneumonia with both my lungs infected badly and the lung capacity for air reduced significantly. It seemed like a very virulent and strong bacterial attack. I was taken to the ICU and a few strong drugs were administered. An oxygen mask was fixed over my nose all the time as my lung capacity had reduced. My husband flew back by late afternoon. Though I was in immense pain I was thankful to God for a timely diagnosis and treatment that would put me back on track. As I lay calmer on my hospital bed, the urge to look at my Blackberry came over me. *Work* had acted like a distraction from the pain I was undergoing. As I scanned through the numerous mails, I felt the need to respond and be a part of the action going on in office. My team members were unaware of what was really going on with me. One mail led to another and I got engrossed with work.

A few days later after consuming various antibiotics, consulting doctors, living on an oxygen mask, and a little Blackberry time, I was given permission to go home as my fever had broken, with my body temperature coming back to normal. Doctors advised complete bed rest for four weeks and only then to resume work, gradually. Happy with the advice, I was relieved to be back home with my children who I had not seen for a while.

My parents, who were scheduled to be in London for a holiday that summer, came in earlier. One really should count one's blessings at such moments! Two days of rest, some good food, some bad medicines, I started to feel life seeping back into me. And then on one of those evenings, I started to feel unwell again with high temperature creeping into my body. Inspite of my limited medical knowledge, I knew that a fever while a patient is on antibiotics is not good news. So the next day I decided to visit my doctor and he put me through an X-ray.

What was about to happen next is not something I had ever imagined or could fathom. My doctor looked at my X-Ray report with an extremely distressed look on his face. He straightened in his chair and then gradually bent forward towards me and said, 'Mrs. Kumar, we need you back in the hospital now!' I heard him but I really did not feel that unwell! Hence I insisted to the doctor that I would like to join my children for dinner and maybe get admitted to the hospital the next morning! After all, I had not spent enough time with the children in the last week. The doctor looked at me again and said, 'Mrs. Kumar, I am sorry but we cannot permit that. You need to be in the hospital now.' The urgency in the tone of his voice made it apparent that something was not quite right and he was not taking a 'no' for an answer. I sat back. My husband and mother requested me to sit in the reception as they got the lowdown. As per the doctor's analysis, my body had become extremely weak given I had not been eating well for months, working silly hours, and clearly, some wine once in a while did not help. The bottom line was that I lived a bad lifestyle. Hence the first bout of malicious pneumonia had weakened the body significantly. Unfortunately, the bacteria had been very virulent. It had somehow developed immunity to my medicines and struck again with more vengeance. I was now struck by a second attack of pneumonia while still recovering from the first one! This could be fatal. My pleural membrane was severely impacted and there was fluid gushing into my lungs, which in a few hours would reduce my ability to breathe significantly! Doctors had to treat me urgently and move me to strongest fifth-generation antibiotics to save my lungs before it was too late. Those medicines were likely to have other impacts on my body which had to be gauged quickly before it was too late. They also had to suck the fluids out of my lungs if I got strong enough to endure that procedure.

He finally gave me an ultimatum – I had forty eight to seventy two hours to live. If the medicines worked, it would be a miracle. The final verdict was to be given only if they could get the infection under control that night!

As my mother broke the news to me, I was petrified. It felt surreal. This couldn't be happening to me! I was the strong woman – wife, mother, daughter and a successful professional. I almost had it all. Destiny has a cruel way of getting you to your knees and telling you how you may not always have it all unless you respect what God has given you.

As we all quietly drove home, it was very tough for me. I was numb. This diagnosis could not sink into my logical brain. Was this really happening to me? I reached home with a heavy heart, packed my bags, yet unsure if I truly was *that* sick. My children Avni and Sid, then nine and five years old respectively, hugged me tight and smiled at me, which made me forget all the pain that I was going through. I explained to the children that I needed to be in the hospital for a few days so that I could be back to play with them soon. Meanwhile the news that their grandmother was going to be with them cheered them up a lot. Children are so innocent that it really hurt that I could not explain the reality to them.

That night when I entered the hospital, little did I know that it would not be easy coming back home. It was almost like the disease was waiting for me to reach the hospital to strike me in an even more forceful way! As I lay in the hospital bed during one of the darkest nights of my life, my fever started to shoot up and in a few hours I had hit a hundred and five degrees Fahrenheit. My consciousness was almost leaving my body. I felt I would explode, my body ached so much that I could not feel my limbs. An excruciating pain had engulfed me. I was put on an ice bed with emergency drips of antibiotics, as the medicines were far too strong to take orally. Even a slight cough felt like a painful explosion in my lungs and I lost a piece of myself every time that happened. By early morning my oxygen levels were shooting down. Multiple tubes were inserted in my body and I continued hoping I would be able to breathe. Blood tests indicated a severe bout of infection. The oxygen mask was back with a bigger cylinder!

Over the next few days, thanks to the medication, I continued to breathe in at a slow pace. The infection became stronger and my body, more frail. I saw my life blurring and slipping away gradually. I had three chest specialists attending to me and in the next seventy-two hours even as the medications became stronger, the infection refused to abate. The infections were competing against the doctors and were winning. My appetite had completely disappeared and in a few days I lost ten pounds as my body braved this onslaught. I was not permitted to get out of my room, as my body was so weak that it would contract any infection in the corridors. After a few days, a blood test indicated traces of septicaemia that made my doctors, family and friends panic. A bout of septicaemia (infection in blood) could be completely fatal at this stage. Given that I was kept completely sanitised, this infection could only be contracted from an infected syringe in the hospital. So the hospital and doctor decided to carry out tests of my entire body to check how deep-seated the infection was. I was in a daze when I was carried from one test lab to another for my own survival. However, there was one particular evening during that time that stood out for me.

I was taken for a bone scan and my body was slipped into a steel chamber (very ironically, the size of a coffin, to be exact) and a steel plate was lowered on my face. A sense of claustrophobia overwhelmed me and I almost choked and felt this was the end. My breathing became even more hurried and I started to mumble and choke with tears rolling down my eyes. The physician sensed my panic-stricken state and asked me to close my eyes and visualise the most important things in my life. In his very calming voice, he told me to focus on what I would do when I get back to my normal self and out of this hospital. I felt so very desperate to do that! I closed my eyes and gradually sunk into my thoughts: two smiling faces flashed before my eyes. My children, Avni and Sid, were looking at me with joy and pure happiness with hope beaming in their eyes. The sun was shining upon their beautiful faces and the playful rays danced about in their hair as the gentle wind caressed their foreheads. Mother Nature was looking after them as their own mother was not around! Their innocent smiles made me want to get up and kiss their faces. They were holding hands and giggling and running on the fresh green grass that was just mowed in the park near our place. Both looked at me and asked, 'Mamma where have you been? We've been missing you!' They were calling me towards them. Suddenly, I saw Sid stumble and fall on a stone and my heart missed a beat. I almost got up to hold him but I could not as I realised I was trapped in the coffin-like chamber – reality sank in and I just could not hold back my tears after that and started to sob with my eyes tightly closed lest I let those smiling faces disappear! An overwhelming guilt came over me. There was so much I had yet to do in life. Had I been too selfish just fulfilling my ambitions? I wanted to walk on the freshly-mowed grass with my children, helping them walk through the obstacles of life. I wanted to spend time cooking their favourite dishes. I wanted to hug them!

I felt incomplete as I felt that I had not delivered on motherhood and somewhere that pull was becoming stronger. I had to teach my children about life and I had hardly done enough of that till now. It became clearer what I needed to do better once I got out of the hospital. I survived that test and the result for septicaemia were negative, much to the relief of all of the medical staff and us. However, the fluids in the lungs increased; so the doctor decided to carry out a procedure one afternoon to salvage me. By then, I was losing my mind in the hospital room. I was told my children were coming to see me in the evening, which kept me in a happy mood during the day. Sometime in the afternoon a big machine was wheeled into my room with two doctors. My mother was with me (who was aware of the procedure) and helped them settle in the room. I was told it was a procedure to review fluids in my lungs, which would be quick. A dose of local anaesthesia was injected – into my bare upper back, making it numb. In a few minutes I found this big machine behind my back and before I could realise, a thick needle was being lowered into my lungs through my back. In spite of the strong anaesthesia I could almost feel that needle going through my rib cage into my lungs, and I screamed with this excruciating pain, with tears rolling down. The doctors were simply doing their job with the machine, pulling out the fluid from my lungs. They wanted to increase the lung capacity and also take samples to test the fluid to gauge the impact of the antibiotic treating the pleural infection. No amount of intellectual justification works when you are in grave pain. All I did then was to plead and beg them to take it off. The procedure took about ten to twelve minutes but they were probably the most excruciating ones in the days that I had been in the hospital so far. I had cried so much that there were no more tears left in my eyes. A sense of apathy and resignation came over. My mother helped me lie down on the bed and I was shivering for a long while, shaken by the experience even though the machine was long gone!

In a few hours my children arrived to meet me. Blissfully unaware about what was really happening with their mom, all they talked to me excitedly about was a friend's upcoming birthday party. My daughter wanted to check as to what she should wear; whereas my son was wondering what gift he'd buy for the friend. My son thought I had such a *cool* life with unlimited TV and unlimited food of any kind that I could ask for whenever I wanted. I smiled and talked to them drearily trying to keep up their excitement. They were gone in an hour but had left me more alive than ever!

Over the next few days I lost more weight and daily blood tests did not indicate any slowdown in the infection. Frustration started to build in the family and me as to why my infection or fever was not breaking. My blood counts went down severely and I found it difficult to walk. Days became weeks, weeks became months and three months passed by!

To keep my sanity I requested the doctors to change my room every week. From leading a hectic 24x7 lifestyle at work and home, I felt grounded and jailed with this illness, which was now beginning to take a toll on my mental well-being. I did not want to lose hope but doubts were beginning to creep in as to when, if ever I would get out. Should I go to another country or hospital for treatment? Should I go beyond the specialists that were attending to me? Nothing can be more frustrating when your mind is fully functional but your body is not co-operating. My heart would break every day when I would see my father buzz with anticipation on test results hoping that they would be better and then see a gush of disappointment when the results came negative. My parents had probably prayed to all their Gods, had sent in sermons from all the gurus they knew, offered votives. Small pleasures of life had suddenly become so important that all I wanted was my normal life back and I did not know how to!

Despair and desolation led me to consult another doctor who we had known through earlier interactions. He suggested going through another diagnostic procedure of bronchoscopy. These entailed tubes with cameras being inserted in my lungs though my nose (while I was awake!) through which my lungs would be washed, fluids extracted and internal pictures taken for analysis to review the treatment. However, whether it was washing of the lungs, earlier medicines or prayers, my fever, miraculously, broke the next day!

Reports started to show improvement with the fever receding and I started to recover over the next few weeks with medicines continuing. Miraculously, I was much better in three weeks and back on my feet. I was in disbelief! It was a miracle...life was giving me a second chance...

When I consulted my doctor on what had happened and how I recovered, I recall him telling me, 'Mrs. Kumar, it does not matter anymore how you got better, what matters is that you are better and healthier, and keep it that way! Look after yourself and lead a holistic life. Your body tells you how much stress it can take. Listen to it!' Since then I always have.

This was the most defining experience of my life till date and I am truly very grateful that I came back from the clutches of death. My family had a key role to play in this. I came back and *did* go to the park with my children, cooked their favourite dishes and played with their toys. I let my husband watch his TV channels in the bedroom, which earlier, was a complete no-no! In a hard way, I learnt the importance of balancing my life with my loved ones and what I loved to do at work. I understood the importance of time spent well and picked up my life all over again. Given the agony my parents had recently gone through due to my illness, I spent some quality time with them over a vacation. There are no words to describe how they would have felt seeing their child slip away. It was a rude awakening about how important it is to take care of oneself. In life, what does not kill you makes you stronger and I think that's what happened to me after this traumatic experience. I became more respectful of personal time, a healthier lifestyle but even more determined to realise my passions at work too! Life teaches you a few lessons in a harsh way if you don't listen to the subtle messages. You need to be brave and keep your chin up.

In my first week of the illness, when I understood that I was in the hospital for a long haul, I called up my office and business heads to apprise them of my state. Everybody at work was obviously very shocked and was extremely supportive. They offered me all the assistance that I may have needed. Given I was unsure of ever coming back to work then, I had to tell the Business Head of Banking to go ahead and hire someone else to ensure continuity of work for him. He knew I was really passionate about what I did at work and we had a wonderful professional relationship. After hearing me, he said, 'Anu, we will not hire anyone in this role. You will be fine and you will come back. We will wait however long this may take. You will be back on your feet and see us through the year-end reviews!' Moments like these give you tremendous strength. These moments are beyond work. I knew that it was a really tough period for the business amidst the financial crisis and without this role being filled in, they would struggle as I am sure they did. But they waited and I went back to work finally, and ran the year-end process. Their confidence in me was stronger than mine. My work was important to me. So I *had* to get back and now I was even emotionally-bound to the banking teams.

PASSION FUELS PERSEVERANCE

When you like something and you are fully committed to it, then you are able to overcome any hardships that stand in your way. Your passion for life, family and work makes your resolve to win even stronger. During my illness and even after that, there were many friends, relatives, and my parents who advised me to take a break or take it easy, given that I had returned from a harsh illness. But would you ever stop living for the fear of dying? My illness taught me to look after myself by eating properly, exercising and having a lot of *me* time, but it also taught me life is short and I needed to speed up and persist on my leadership journey. Most importantly, it taught me to spend time wisely with family. There is a time for everything in life!

WORK ON YOURSELF HOLISTICALLY

My mother once told me that I can have it all for some time and some of it all the time but *couldn't* have all of it, all the time! As I recovered from my illness, I resolved to challenge this notion and continue to aspire to have it all, so long as I knew what 'all' meant to me and I had planned a path to get there! We all play multiple roles of a mother, wife, daughter, employee, manager and so on. This is not different from what our male counterparts do. However, what sets us apart are the varied expectations and the social norms that guide women. A woman is expected to be the care-giver and many times that role supersedes most other things she would like to do. As I grew up, I had various men and women who were role models around me at school, college, home and at work. Each one had different drivers that made them happy. But more men looked after themselves physically and psychologically, which helped them juggle multiple balls at the same time and get the best of different worlds. The nurturing streak of most women somehow makes them neglect their own well-being, which is critical to happiness.

When I was unwell I craved to get back on my two feet. It was hugely frustrating to want something physically and emotionally and your body not being able to deliver it. The feeling of helplessness was immense. Though I knew intellectually that health is wealth, it had never really sunk in until this phase of critical illness. Through this experience, I learnt the importance of monitoring my health with regular check-ups, exercise and healthy food. A lot of this is clichéd, but in my experience I know a lot of women who put themselves on the back burner on this aspect.

Also, after this experience I learnt that the value and equity we create holds us in good stead in trying times. The organisation and my business stakeholders stood behind me as steady as a rock in this tough experience. Was this because they simply liked my work? Or was it because I was someone they thought needed help? I would like to believe that this was because they saw true value in what I brought to the table. It was also because they knew that I would not quit mid-way or give up. My courage may flounder but would certainly not fall short in trying times!

SUMMARY

The common thing across all heroic stories is the intensity of struggle they entail. And the panacea to all these struggles is also common, like the courage exhibited by the protagonist. I view this journey as a life film, full of twists and turns that allow you a chance to emerge successfully. Having witnessed multiple such ups and downs, I feel that each turn provides an opportunity to succeed and leaves you richer with stronger shades of courage. So, if you have clarity of purpose and are convinced that you can achieve it, the next step is to make your choice and fill your armoury with arrows of courage and march on:

- Courage to pursue your dreams: by having faith in who you are and by trusting your intuition and your judgment – Staying on course and doing what you love gives you a true sense of joy, but also requires you to be tough in the face of adversity. It is akin to climbing a mountain in face of stormy weather without wearing yourself down. This takes effort and mental strength.

- Courage to deal with biases – be it a cultural bias, a gender bias or any stereotype that you fit in – it can be dealt with creating awareness and facing fallouts with courage. If you think through carefully, these biases are another's roadblock that you are helping them cross and not really an issue that you bring to the table. So don't let self-doubt crop up. Look at the situation objectively to identify the trigger. If you see merit in bringing the issue upfront, do it. If you feel it is better to mould yourself without losing your integrity, adapt. Have the courage to change and manoeuvre through the course.

- Courage to take risks – Never underestimate your own capability. A war is first won from within. So, instead of choosing an easy way out, choose what gives you the required growth to reach your destination. Sometimes pursuing your dreams will entail taking bets and risks in life. Thinking about the worst that could happen and then gauging if it is as *bad* will help you move forward.

- Courage to see through the unforeseen – Know that there will be instances beyond your control, persevere and keep the desire to resurface. Your will to stay, give miracles a reason to show up.

- Life teaches us the lessons that we tend to ignore. There is life beyond work too. We all wish to live life at its fullest. Don't let the stress and hardship take over your being. Prevention is always better than cure, so adopt a healthier lifestyle to see it through. Without physical health, we cannot really deliver what our mind really wants to do. Whenever we skew too much towards any one dimension of life and ignore others, it kicks us hard to set us right. We need to have the strength and a brave mind to deal with it.

5 CONFIDENCE
the key to managing competition

CONFIDENCE

'With confidence, you have won before you have started.'
– Marcus Garvey

Confidence is about self-belief, in accordance with one's skills, competencies and capabilities. This self-belief has to reflect in the way one communicates, behaves and earns the trust and respect of people around him. What we say and how we say it has to be congruent with our body language, tone and expressions. A passionate and purpose-driven approach helps one keep their confidence level up, even when faced with roadblocks. Speaking from experience, I feel that in the face of adversity, this inner strength will never let us succumb to any failure. Your confidence in yourself will help you pick yourself up, dust yourself off and run again. This is not always easy and it requires self-awareness and a pulse of the external environment. This enables one to be adaptive to various changes and stakeholders without being distracted from core values and beliefs.

Ascending up the ladder poses tough challenges. Similar to moving from the shallows of a river to the depths of an ocean, the new environment, at times, may feel intimidating. I also believe that the problem and the solution reside in our mind. How you are able to hold your own defines the length and success of your journey. What keeps you going is your inner strength, conviction and confidence, and the extent to which you believe in your own competence and the confidence to feel deserving of every achievement.

MANAGING POLITICS

The great teacher and philosopher, Plato has said, 'One of the penalties for refusing to participate in politics is that you end up being governed by your inferiors.'

Well, while *inferiors* might appear to be a strong term in today's context, it could well be replaced by *those who may not be better-suited or more capable*! Be savvy and confident to manage both the good and bad at work.

How does this really relate to women? Whether at work or at home, women are always juggling multiple priorities at the same time. Deadlines at work, deadlines in children's schools, meals, birthday parties and so on – we manage it all to the best of our ability! However, when it comes to managing the work environment, research tells us that many women, especially at senior-to-mid levels, find it difficult to navigate the organisational corridors of the complicated matrices. Organisations, by definition, have inter-personal dynamics between people working together. These dynamics, laced with certain intent, could be called politics. These mazes have to be efficiently navigated through to accomplish the appropriate goals, which we set for ourselves.

I have some experience observing women in this respect vis-a-vis men and have found out that even the most competent of women employees struggle to manage organisational politics. It is where their confidence (or lack of it) leads to, and at other times, it is a result of their unwillingness to even acknowledge the existence of and need for managing this space! Successful women leaders learn to steer through this navigation much earlier in their career. They learn to think, strategise and execute.

One of the reasons for this is that often, many women tend to believe that managing harmonious relationships at work is the answer. Keeping this intact at the cost of self-deprivation creates stress. In the conflicting game of chess at the workplace, women often overarch to keep peace and preserve relationships at any cost, even though it may translate to sacrificing themselves or their interests. Their need to be seen as caring, nurturing and a peacemaker can drive them to a tipping point beyond endurance. In such situations, I have had some of my women colleagues bow out of the leadership race. They had decided that it may not be worth continuing work with such hardships. There was a feeling of helplessness and the dissonance of adopting styles not very familiar to them. Given the stress of politics, these colleagues were more comfortable being at home with their family rather than deal with stressful conflicts at work.

These conflicts, however, are a part of the journey towards leadership, both for women *and* men. Leaving work at such junctures, may sometimes take away from women what might have been rightfully theirs. Managing organisational politics is not about doing anything unethical but about acknowledging and managing human dynamics properly. In any organisational environment, there are likely to be cliques, friends, acquaintances, and some foes. From what I've gathered from my experience, one has to study the environment and understand where and how one fits in. Then, pick a circle of trust and have close associates, followed by acquaintances. Even the ones who seem unlikely to be your close associates should be kept very close! The most important bit is to be aware of what goes on around you. Often individuals may get set up in a complex quagmire of problems because they're completely unaware of the games being played behind their back! Pardon my saying this, but it is almost like having another pair of eyes on your back. Your allies and close associates help you with it. Women need to step up to the game in this aspect!

It is also important to think ahead and keep the big picture in mind. This will usually help you evaluate the different people you are interacting with at work. You may need to anticipate who might be satisfied or not as you move forward on certain initiatives. By looking at the big picture and the players in it, you can apprehend peoples' response and be ready for appropriate intervention in case someone stumps you.

It also helps to validate your actions from time to time. Ask for feedback from people you work with, as one may have blind spots that need uncovering! While two minds are often better than one, bear in mind that not all feedback is accurate so you do need to apply your judgment and balance the feedback with your own conviction. Review relevant stakeholder feedback that you need to address. Manage it constructively and sensitively. Some feedback is data-driven while others may be perception-driven. Perceptions are not realities but they drive people's behaviour towards you.

As you grow, there are bound to be people who will be very happy with your success and a few who may not be. Those unhappy people may be apprehensive of your progression (after all, there are limited seats at the top) and may also react negatively to you at work. These interactions are inevitable and depending on your situation, you can choose to ignore them, or deal with them. Dealing with such people, however, requires you to understand and empathise with them first. It is possible that you can convert them into allies by partnering on common goals. This is an option you should certainly explore. It is also likely that you may not ever become friends with them, as they may not be comfortable with you or with your ideas. In such a case, it is best to let them move on. However, be aware and cautious. You can manage your alliances at work to know of any harm that might be directed towards you. Some of these people can diffuse negative energy, which can be vicious at times. If you allow this to take over, it has the potential to destroy your good work. Hurtful words and gossip are reflection of other people's insecurities and you have to remain calm and objective if you ever come across such situations. You need to be vigilant but also have to insulate yourself mentally to not let this impact you or distract you from your path. It is a must to ensure that your alliances across levels are keeping you strong. Being lonely in such situations can be tough. Reach out to your network for support during such moments.

In one of my assignments, my bias for action was perceived 'pushy' even though it was client-centric and driven with much energy. This created some discomfort amongst some members of my working group. Within my group of peers everyone knew that I was taking the right decision and direction, however few would rise to the occasion to help me manage the political dynamics. There were not-so-noble motives ascribed to my actions at times. I tried to change the style and behaviours to garner better support and improvise on perceptions. However very often, even though one may make systematic changes to one's behaviour, people around them don't let memories die. I understood that these issues exist and one cannot shy away from them; they have to be dealt with appropriately and head on, which eventually accelerates you on the path to your goal. Running away does not! During these periods a few credible allies in the internal network in the function helped me. These were trusted relationships that I had built over regular interactions and they were the critical anchor points of support when I faced challenging situations at work. They would provide me with feedback and the needed advice about people that I was dealing with. This helped me keep my confidence in my peer relationships and actions as I managed that assignment.

SOCIAL CONDITIONING AT WORK CAN IMPACT CONFIDENCE

Men and women have a persona prescribed to how a woman should behave, work, socialise and so on. Most times, this persona prescribed is that of a polite, gentle nurturing woman, and certainly not assertive and ambitious!

Hence if one is found atypical by being straightforward, direct, standing her ground at times, there could be some dissonance. I felt this conflict with both men and women around me. I felt some of them (not all) almost wanted to hold me back and force-fit me into being something I was not. Being forward-looking in getting work done was termed '*aggressive*' which was not a positive attribute for a woman. If I focused on client deliverables more than the norm, it was then termed as being self-centered and not collaborative. I understood the art of managing and balancing internal and external demand, but I also had to battle these perceptions and not let them break me down. It took a lot of inner strength. I had to keep myself focused on my purpose. This could work in different ways.

Sometimes as women progress to leadership roles, they have to step out of the socially defined box and speak up for themselves. In one instance, one of my women colleagues, was a successful banker and was rated 'exceptional' on the basis of her business performance. She had performed her previous role for many years and it had been her comfort zone. An ambitious individual, she had set her focus on a larger role that was vacant. She was offered the role, on the basis of her proven performance, potential to carry bigger roles and her own preference to do this.

A few months down the line, it all started to fall apart, and I saw it unfolding in front of me. I tried to quickly assess what was really going wrong to help her resurrect. She had lost senior stakeholder's confidence, the team's confidence as well as her own. I could see her trying hard, but something was not falling into place. A closer look through executive assessment confirmed my initial views wherein a great performer was struggling to transition into being a leader, as she was not sure how to navigate through the new environment. In spite of performing the larger role she continued to be shy of being vocal amongst the management committees, conflict situations, or in debates with regional stakeholders. Her confidence, which was evident through her technical capability in the previous role, was not being carried through as she climbed the next rung up the ladder. Like most women, she tried to pacify herself and make peace in such situations, where the need for her was to push her way and stick her flag in the ground on her vision and strategy. Her team expected her to take a position for the right reason in tricky business situations, which was not forthcoming.

We helped this leader with the appropriate coaching for a few months. She underwent a lot of introspection and realigned her style to suit the need of her new role. She found her voice but had to overcome her instinctive behaviour that had been positively reinforced over years, to be cordial and talk less. She was uncomfortable pushing back some conflicts in her earlier days; however, the more she did, the easier it became. It took her a lot of effort to deal with this change as she had to make some significant changes in her dealings as a leader. The most important bit was being aware of what was working and what was not. Finally, she was able to make the transition and stand up to some of the tougher calls her role demanded.

COMPETITION MANIFESTS IN MANY WAYS!

'Culture makes people understand each other better. And if they understand each other better in their soul, it is easier to overcome the economic and political barriers. But first they have to understand that their neighbour is, in the end, just like them, with the same problems, the same questions.'
– Paulo Coelho

Bring together people from different cultures, communities, backgrounds, genders and you have the recipe for a whole lot of different interpretations and challenges!

I am reminded of the year 2009, one of the toughest I ever faced. After my prolonged illness which I fought bravely and survived, I returned to work at the London office, which was something that probably gave me more peace than hospital rooms and was one of the core reasons of my existence.

I came back to office and started working towards the annual performance management and compensation process, which was an intensive piece of work at the year-end. Being back at work felt great. However, during that year, there had been structural changes in the team and I had a new manager, Joe*.

Joe had a different style than that of the team members and the business heads. He was a very experienced, seasoned and inetlligent person but was not very engaged at work. Joe's urge to be promoted further, contradicted by his lack of engagement led to not so strong relationships with the business. This resulted in some problematic dynamics in the office. Unfortunately, his limited connect in the office started to impact the team members' productivity, who were struggling with the workload and business issues in times of huge changes in Financial Services. Gradually, this evolved into cliques being formed within the team for support and the environment got a bit dysfunctional. Business started to disengage with the function as well and Joe was not happy with that situation. He was not willing to take the burden of the responsibility for some of these issues. As for me, we had not worked too long together and he had assumed that when I was unwell, business stakeholders would go in for a change and he could have someone more aligned to him, but things did not go in that direction. The business did not want the change. Unknowingly, I became one of the scapegoats of this conflict!

Oblivious to all the politics, cliques, dynamics, I was focused on my priorities at work and home. At work, I gave myself fully and worked diligently on the initiatives and tasks at hand. This gave me tremendous joy. Also, given the turmoil in the financial industry, the business was undergoing a large restructuring, which had kept me hugely busy with new structure in the organisation, design, and various changes in leadership. I was so immersed in my work that I completely overlooked keeping an eye on what may be transpiring behind me or around me in the function that could soon impact me significantly. I did not realise that ignoring the politics around me was the biggest mistake I was making then. Being an ostrich and burying yourself in work does not necessarily protect you from the knives around you. I did not anticipate that the knife would go down my back so smoothly that I would not even realise the harm. Given the subtle dynamics around me, my denial to be a part of it all was a mistake in hindsight and has been one of my key learnings till date! It was not that I was doing everything right but I missed the gap between my manager and the business I supported. I missed that he felt the need for a change or alignment. It did not dawn on me that I needed to reach out to allies or my network for support or feedback. This oversight impacted me in a way that I had not anticipated.

That year I was due for a promotion and I felt confident that on the basis of my hard work in the role, I deserved it. My mid-year feedback had been good with my earlier manager and also with head of the function. I had been doing an enhanced role for two years and had been a key partner with some of the businesses in the transformation that was undertaken during the financial crisis and delivered successfully. Thus I felt well-positioned for the elevation.

On the day of the promotion announcements in January, I anxiously waited for my turn to get the phone call from our HR Head's office. Usually we got such calls by mid-day, so the excitement was building up. At about 4 pm, one of my colleagues, Jane* who was also being considered for the promotion that year, got the call. Time ticked on and I waited for my turn. She returned with a rather puzzled expression on her face. When I quizzed her about the promotion bit, she was quite evasive and rushed into her room on the pretext of making an urgent call, which was rather strange!

Anyway, I was called in next. I headed towards the HR Head's office, with butterflies in my stomach, some excitement and anticipation in my heart. However when I met him, he had a slightly troubled expression on his face. He handed me a letter, which had my bonus for the year. I thanked him for the same and waited for him to go further, and then he fumbled. He said that I was a very talented individual but as per the promotion process, there was some development feedback with regards to how I worked with my manager and some of the other team members hence my promotion was deferred! There had been some impact on the overall team delivery and some of this was attributed to me. He further said that I needed to work on these aspects and hopefully with this being sorted, things would fall in place next year.

He finally finished with a sense of relief creeping on his face after delivering the bad news that he had been struggling with.

I was shocked! I looked at him again and asked him if he was serious. Across the HR floor, within my team, in my business, I was aware that there was an impression and expectation of the promotion given my role and tenured performance. I could not comprehend what really happened here. He continued and apprised me that others, including Jane, had got promoted. I felt something must be horribly wrong with me. I think he expected the reaction and was ready with his calming response for that moment, which made no sense to me at that time.

I felt disappointed and didn't know how to exit his office. I had lost a lot of my self confidence in that moment. In that emotional state, I thought this was unfair. Post my illness, I had worked hard, managed some of the toughest clients, toughest situations, kept all out of turmoil, straddling across a very challenging transformation, but clearly that was not enough. The perception of how one managed some relationships had an overwhelming weightage for the decision. The function Head, in his usual amicable demeanour, probably told me the unsaid, as to how I had not managed the internal environment and perceptions well enough with my manager or peers. This had created a hindrance for me to move ahead to the next level. Call it politics, organisational dynamics, or not-so-aligned managers, the loss was entirely mine This was a dark moment in my career when my confidence in my own capabilities wavered.

In retrospect, I was so unnecessarily emotional about this incident that I thought about moving on from the organisation. At that time, this had hurt my pride somewhere. The Function Head refused to accept my resignation and requested me to calm down, knowing very well that it was a reaction taken without much thought. Some forty five minutes later, I headed down to my office to collect my bag. On the way I called my husband who understood my agony and told me he would be there shortly to pick me up. His presence was extremely comforting and we headed home together. Over the late evening I simply avoided any calls from office. My shock turned to curious anger by the next morning. How could I let this happen to me? What did I miss? What did I really get wrong? All the right questions in my head – albeit a bit late. I tried to pull myself together that morning, debating whether to go to the office or not. This is where my husband stepped in firmly and asked me to look at this problem in its face and take charge. I picked up myself and headed to work which was the step forward.

I found it difficult to resurrect myself and trust the system, initially. Over the next few days, I experienced some dissonance that took over my usual rational being. Unfortunately I got a bit myopic and probably somewhat obsessed with the sense of unfairness I had faced that demotivated me. Unfair maybe it was, but was it worth this much emotional energy? Did I have a role to play in this? Maybe yes, maybe I could have managed the environment, managers and some peers better! I felt torn between the stakeholders.

During this tough professional experience, what I did realise is the tremendous equity and constructive relationship that I held with a lot of people that I worked with. It overwhelmed me in a positive way. Many well-wishers, mentors and friends extended their support and vote of confidence. I did not consider myself that important, so this came as a pleasant surprise! Finally we reached a conclusion wherein I agreed that it was best for me to undergo a transition coaching to understand what was the appropriate way forward.

ORGANISATION SAVVY

At this juncture, along with my coach, I identified a few friends and associates, who were more approachable and supportive in helping me find my feet again. My coach and buddies taught me how to understand the environment and not bury oneself in work. They coached me to interpret the subtle cues, importance of small talk and how perception had an important role to play in people's behaviour towards self. That coaching was transformational and an eye-opener. As a part of this intervention, for a 360 feedback, I chose people, whom I had a good relationship with and some people with whom I shared a not-so-good relationship, while a few who were neutral. A wholesome feedback from a variety of people including stakeholders, team and peers was very helpful and telling. Some of this feedback was constructive whereas some of it was brutal. But feedback is a gift and I took it in the right spirit to address what I rightly could. It was amazing to see some generic comments about what some people thought of me without knowing me well. For example: she is too assertive in her conduct. On further probing I understood that some non-verbal cues that I may be displaying in a different environment or with a few people may be leading to this. What may be acceptable by some may be perceived in a different light by others. I understood the importance of alignment (not keeping neutral), while continually scanning the workplace about who was an ally and who was not. So the challenges for a South-Asian Woman in the West are multi-layered indeed!

On a positive note, there were the encouraging bits about commercial acumen and high action bias that I was advised to continue doing. A key and consistent feedback was to be more organisationally savvy by managing different relationships with different styles while keeping oneself authentic. Complicated! But therein came the development action plan in place and a huge effort on my part to keep trying to do this.

I realised that it did not matter what my intent was, what I did or how I did it. It was how others perceived it that guided their reaction and impressions towards me. I was culturally different and probably had a different style. So was this a cultural variance even though this issue was limited to a group? It dawned upon me that I did need to make some changes to my behaviour for perceptions to change.

There were certain things I had to work on like engaging and reaching out more to a larger work group, having coffee or lunch when feasible to build informal relationships. I was an introvert and this did not come naturally to me. It was difficult to explain it to others. I had to force myself to reach out and that helped people understand me better. They understood that I really *did* mean well and wanted to be inclusive. This was easier for people to see when I met them face-to-face. It was tough in the beginning to break the ice with people as various team members had a view about how I conducted myself at work but also were unclear about what they could expect from me.

Over the next few months, I redirected my energy to managing internal relationships more appropriately. I did not fundamentally change myself but I altered the way I interacted with others in the team around me. That did make a huge difference.

However, a few people refused to change their views, irrespective of what I did. I could never win over some, as they had strong views based on their own experiences in life that were beyond me. However, being aware about this helped me to deal with them appropriately by having objective, work-related discussions when we were in the same working group. I reconciled to it and decided to be a little more watchful. Over a period of time, I cultivated some strong friendships that were tremendously helpful. Given that I had an honest intent which was then apparent, things became easier at work. During this period, my confidence in my own abilities was greatly restored.

Things started to fall into place. I further imbibed the habit of making great allies and associates by simply having regular interactions over coffee or lunches. That gradually moved from just work-related discussions to children and home-related chats and relationships grew stronger. I cherish those relationships till date. The promotion did come along the way but by then I had moved to another level of human connections already. That was my biggest achievement and learning. Promotion did not matter that much after it. I realised that I had vested too much energy into something which may not be as significant. I understood that one cannot let competition and rivalry get the best of oneself. What Eleanor Roosevelt said couldn't be truer: 'No one can make you feel inferior without your consent.'

THE NEED TO ASK AND TO BE EXPLICIT ABOUT WHAT YOU DESERVE

I have often seen that many women struggle to seek advice as they constantly hesitate to put a foot in the door for a dialogue on their next career move. They expect others to recognise their work and feel uncomfortable about proactively talking about their achievements or networking. In this competitive age, it is increasingly important to be able to articulate your accomplishments to an evolving opportunity as you grow within your organisation. In a tough environment, where rules are often rewritten, you need to be prepared with your support structure to take on the challenge and explore the depths of the corporate world.

In my experience and also having reviewed some research, what is important for women is nurturance and acceptance by others to earn what they deserve. There is an unsaid expectation wherein women feel if they work diligently and display commitment, their manager should recognise them and reward them appropriately without them having to ask for it. It is not in the DNA of many women to ask for their dues or demand what they feel they truly deserve. Many a time this leads to a skewed situation wherein the manager may think the employee is content with what she has, when that *might* not be the case. Rewards or compensation is limited in any company and the prioritisation may be done according to the performance, risk and any legitimate employee tasks.

I find that the unmet, muted expectations are one of the main reasons why few women stay in the corporate world and fewer make it to the top. Generally speaking, most people face a situation when one of the partners need to take their career with some flexibility while the other pursues it seriously to keep the financial security.

There are times when it is the women who take the back seat voluntarily. It may not be on others' insistence. This is driven partly by social norms where generations have been groomed to view females as nurturers and men, the earners as stated earlier; but a lot of it is their own mindset. This does not really help to build confidence at work. Hence, even in the absence of a dire need to resign from their careers, women willingly give up even before attempting to even try the balancing act, just because there's no unsaid insistence from the world around to prove themselves and they may have chosen not to be the bread earner. There may not be an easy solution to this apart from more women getting out there and being confident and persistent.

It has been often debated how women struggle to ask for the right money or promotion for the work they do. Some know that they are underpaid compared to their predecessor or for the job they do; however, I have seen women struggle with asking for what is due. I have been on both sides of the table and I feel if you don't ask, you don't get. Niceties are important and such discussions have to be managed appropriately. But not asking because you may be unsure how it impacts a relationship or how it will be perceived cannot be a driver. I have also seen that sometimes, maybe unconsciously, a woman's partner having a career, may impact how such decisions may be viewed, especially in emerging markets, where such information is easily available and usually a woman's income is considered secondary to her husband's.

Women have to get over the discomfort of asking for their due as there is no special art of doing this. It is a simple discussion about what you do, how you add value, where you think the market is, assess your benchmarks and then leave it for your manager to explain why you are still underpaid and what he or she is going to do about this. Keep the discussion objective without blaming anyone. Highlight your contributions and what you do. Talk about your commitment to the company, but also subtly talk about how the system should not take that for granted. If you are valuable and the company wants to retain you, they would do what is appropriate. If they don't, you have to really think hard if this is the right place for you. Working women have a tough life and work is no charity. Underselling yourself is a disservice to yourself. If you don't have confidence in yourself and know what you are worth, there is little chance that anyone else will.

I have seen some women very emotive on such issues and messing up such discussions. Emotions block our reasoning and may mar our behaviours or dialogues to manage an issue constructively. Very often such women have waited long for a senior to recognise them for their commitment, dedication or hard work and when that did not happen there was a repeated plea. Finally, cynicism took over and the conversation went awry! If you have asked for what you deserve appropriately and it does not come by, preserve your self-respect and look for better options. It is important to manage these interactions objectively and with grace and dignity. Do not let these situations bruise your confidence!

After moving overseas in a new role, a colleague of mine was given an offer which she felt was below the market and also lesser than the previous incumbent. There was some dissonance in her mind and she decided speak to her manager about it with the data in hand. The manager understood and agreed with her thinking but explained his limitation on budgets. To this, she offered that she was willing to take the role if this was corrected in the coming six to eight months. They agreed and she took up the offer. Sometimes being sensitive to the constraints and helping work the situations through can become a win-win.

In Singapore or Europe, which has a more subtle culture, one had to fine-tune navigation through the environment and the people around. Unlike me, many women pick up subtleties better and at times I have found them more perceptive of the moods of others than their male counterparts. That is something I feel can be a real strength for women and worth fine-tuning to be used in different situations.

EVERY INDIVIDUAL HAS SOME STRENGTHS, AND SOMETHING TO LEARN FROM EVERYONE!

The one indulgence I have pampered myself with has been to observe and imbibe from successful individuals around me. Many a time, we get caught up in trying to find a role model who has almost all the qualities that we deem inspirational that we feel we can learn from. If you can find a role model, then that is wonderful. However, my mantra has been to learn from all people around me to build our learning and confidence.

Many people around you are doing a few things really well, notice those closely and see if it aligns to your value system and your way of doing things. This can propel you forward faster if you imbibe it. I remember that a senior business head (a man) whom I worked with, no matter what problem you took to him, one always walked out feeling great and confident about what was going on. I started to reflect on this closely and wanted to understand how I could replicate it. After all, how can you go wrong with making people feel good about themselves? After some deep reflections, I realised that in all my interactions, he was making me feel as if I was key to his plan and was critical to solving the problem at hand even though he was quietly sowing the seeds of solution in my mind. This person made me feel that I was creating tremendous value, which was commendable. Now, who would not feel good about that? It made me realise, that around me, there were many such individuals who were probably coming to me for similar problem-solving interactions. I replicated my experience and worked on making them feel really good about their efforts no matter how small or big. It was miraculous, individual commitment increased, productivity rocketed and there was cheer around me. I used to feel self-assured and confident when dealing with this leader. This made me realise as I grew through the rungs, it was also critical for me to build the confidence of those who worked with me!

Another instance of learning and confidence-building was when I worked with a senior in Asia. He was always three steps ahead of everyone else with any plan or issue. That was remarkable because we were always prepared for any exigency. On closer observation, I realised that he had the uncanny ability of looking at the big picture and was connecting multiple dots and systems together while analysing the impact of one plan against another. This resulted in many permutations and combinations in his head for various situations and he could see clearly which solution helped him and hence we (his team) were prepped better. Maybe he was gifted, but the self-assurance he demonstrated had to be a function of his self-confidence. Having seen his operating and analytical style, I tried imbibing some of it and it has really helped me and my team prep for the future. It made us forward-looking, which has been tremendously helpful at work.

There is also learning in observing what is not working. There was a leader I once worked with who was very intelligent, but a bit too analytical and indecisive. With him, we always got caught with paralysis by analysis! His hunt for numbers and data was endless and with no decision at the end. This led to a huge dissatisfaction for people who worked with him. He would deliberate a lot whereas in certain crises, he needed to act quicker. He always followed a highly consensus-driven approach that would work well in a business-as-usual environment but not when there was a crisis at hand. From this interaction, I learnt the value of relying on my intuition and taking timely decisions. Sometimes there will be bets that may go right, sometimes wrong, but we move forward. Leadership is about taking a view with the team and then having the confidence to execute. Strategy and execution go hand-in-hand!

LEARNING OUTSIDE OFFICE

One key aspect to broaden your confidence and keep your learning journey exciting is by doing things outside work. A childhood hobby should be something which we never grow out of. Sports, languages, art and social work help us develop multiple perspectives and give us the outlook to view at things differently. Again, it is clichéd but I would encourage you to look around you and think about how many women you see pursuing hobbies, especially sports. I have found that in my career, engaging with social work and sometimes painting or writing helps me relax, get in touch with my inner self and touches certain chords in my heart that help me feel calmer and grounded. This also stimulates my creative brain and sometimes I think of some of the out-of-the-box new ideas while am not doing the regular work, but unwinding with some of these other activities.

A lot of my thinking and learning also happens while I travel, and my job requires me to travel a lot. I could get bogged down by the disruption it causes sometimes but I choose to be happier about it and look at how I can add to myself with it and the flexibility it provides me with. First and foremost, it forces me to manage my time better as I have no choice but to be organised. With my children's school, and sometimes my husband travelling too, a whole week's timetable for all meals is made in advance with the nanny. This helps me manage weekly groceries and shopping. All school sessions, activities are planned and I would have my parents, friends or nanny stand in if required. I also organise my work better. I ensure the focus does not get diluted and that my work and home priorities go hand-in-hand.

Aside of testing my organising skills, I make the most of my travel. Apart from doing work, I try and reach out to some known friends, professional bodies or associates in the city. If it is a new place, then I tend to explore it. All this adds to your network, and the continuous broadening of your horizons.

SURPRISES IN STORE

Life has a way of turning around and surprising you. This has been true for me whenever I thought I had hit a wall. Then the magic happens...beautiful and unprecedented.

Being able to maintain confidence in oneself, our family, friends and organisation allows us to deal with the unprecedented with a spring in our step.

During times of change in personal or professional circumstances, you need to be confident to take on these changes optimistically, especially if it disrupts the existing harmony on the home or work front. The desire to keep life running like well-oiled machinery all the time may be strong and may make you want to compromise on exposure or growth. Standing up for yourself, having the confidence in yourself is critical and requires a concerted resilience and tremendous energy!

MOVING ON...

The year 2010 turned a new leaf, bringing the much needed change in our lives after the illness and the promotion fiasco. I worked on my development needs and got promoted, focused on my health, which made me physically and mentally stronger.

On the family front, my children had got admissions into some really good schools in London then. As we all know, school entrances are probably more gruelling for parents of young children and that was a real relief. Further, my husband got a new, bigger role with another firm. However, the only problem was that took him back to India. We debated the decision of his job change and decided collectively it may be better for us to return to India given our young children will get an opportunity to be exposed to their roots. Also, I decided to review options externally and internally. We thought we were all set!

In June, 2010, I decided to speak to my manager who was not very happy about my looking for a transfer to India, given that professionally I was well-settled again. Post all the efforts in coaching I had integrated myself back in the function as appropriate. I appreciated his calm yet troubled reaction. His appreciation of our personal circumstances was thoughtful and he agreed to help me out. My next conversation was to be with my seniors, co-heads of Corporate and Investment Bank. This was tougher for me as these seniors had stood by me through my professional and personal struggles in the last twelve months. I was aware that the business was not in great shape, especially because of immense internal and external changes. Somehow I felt torn and conflicted, although going back was the right decision for us as a family.

SHOULD I? OR SHOULD I NOT?

I fumbled through my chat with the seniors as they were not just stakeholders but also my friends. They seemed shocked and requested me to rethink if it was possible for me to be around for six to eight months more so that the ship was a little more stable. Given the heavy restructuring and attrition, there was lack of continuity on the people side. I saw a huge opportunity to be a part of the transformational project that I so wanted to do! It also provided me the much-needed opportunity to reciprocate the support from this business during my illness. Nevertheless, it was an extremely tough decision. My husband and I discussed this, as I had never done this before. He asked me if I *really* wanted to do this and when I said yes, he was behind me like a rock.

I was very nervous not just because my husband would be as far as in India, but, in a few months, my children would follow him. Living just by myself was a daunting task. I must have *really* wanted to do what I was doing and hoped this short-term call would hopefully hold me in a good stead for my learning in the long term.

My mother thought I had really lost my mind given I had recently recovered from a near-fatal illness. She was completely flummoxed by the decision and tried dissuading me. Ultimately, seeing me determined, she decided to support me and comforted me by assuring me that she would be there back home with my family while I would work through my career aspirations. My husband's confidence in my abilities to take this on was a tremendous support, gradually making me more self-assured that I could actually do it.

The Bank stepped up too by giving me all the needed support to live in London and the flexibility to travel to India, as and when required. I leveraged their generosity carefully as I was here to work and learn.

Weeks became months and months went on to become a year. I had signed up for six months and went on to stay for eighteen months travelling every two weeks between London and Delhi. My children learnt to play hide and seek with their mother. The toughest part used to be when I used to leave Delhi to return to London. My son was seven years old at that time and not old enough to understand what was really going on, even though my parents and his father were around. I remember one late night when I was packing my bag to catch the flight back, my son stood next to me, teary-eyed, almost about to sob. My heart just shrank as I knew that tender, lonely and sad expression was because he knew I would be gone in a few hours to be seen only after two to three weeks.

He said, 'Mamma, I need help.'

'My baby! What happened? Tell mamma'. He knew my work was important to me, so he did not ask me not to travel. He murmured, 'Mamma, I have a very sad feeling in my heart and I am getting tears in my eyes! I don't know why. Please help me!' My heart started to cry. I knew the sad feeling that he was unable to express properly, was the anxiety he was experiencing as I was going. I felt, maybe I was being selfish and doing the wrong thing. The guilt overwhelmed me.

I hugged him and asked him to think about our upcoming holiday next month. I told him to get a list ready of all the things that he wanted, what we would do together on the holiday and so on. I lay next to him that night for hours till he went to sleep. I cried on my way to the airport. It is rarely easy for a working mother in such situations. There are no right or wrong answers. My husband held my hand in the car and assured me he would be fine the next day. Children usually have feelings that they do not know how to be explicit about; however, mothers can feel their joy and their pain. And the pain was very much real.

At moments like these, one finds their clarity, conviction, courage and confidence sorely tested. There were these tough moments for me to manage. My daughter who joined mid school in India underwent a huge cultural change and also some bullying in her new school. On one my visits, I realised her self-confidence was impacted. I called office and decided to take three weeks off and be with her in school, spending time with her teachers and peers. My intervention helped her and she regained herself-confidence.

Because I was sure that I was adding value back at work, I had the confidence to ask for the flexibility I required on the personal front.

Once between some hectic work issues, I called at the usual 3 pm India time to talk to the children, who returned from school at this hour. To my shock, I found my son had been suffering from high fever that day and had to be picked up from school. He was rushed to the doctor and diagnosed with viral fever. With the high temperature, he had been clinging to my mother. My heart was in my mouth. As I Skyped home and my mother made me talk to him to assure me that he was okay, a gloom of guilt overtook me. My conscience kept questioning me if I was doing the right thing by being in London as my child suffered at home. I booked my flight that night to go back to Delhi. However, by evening my husband who was back home, called and pacified me for an hour, saying Sid was better, and there he was smiling at me from the computer screen. I almost wanted to jump through the screen and hold him! The chat with my husband helped and Sid was fine in a few days and back to school. I finished my projects and went back home to be welcomed by his beaming smile. He was fine and waiting for his mamma.

As we know, children do get unwell and it is tough, but they do get well soon enough. They need to have close family around them. As a mother, you are their support but so are their father, and grandparents. Let your emotions and responsibilities be shared by others as well. You should of course do what you can but don't kill yourself wth guilt...it does not help. The lesson I learned through this process was also that it is important to have confidence in each other's ability to help one another. We can't do everything alone!

Working across two time zones requires a support system both at work and at home. At work, I had a great assistant, a wonderful team that stood by me and helped me with my schedules. Given my good relationship with the business, they accepted my working flexibly across two-time zones and also aligned themselves to my schedule, for which I was truly grateful.

At home, having a very supportive husband and the unrelenting support of my parents kept me going. We leveraged technology heavily as a family, with Skype, Face Time coming to our aid most of the time. I would Skype the children when they were back from school and from time-to-time help with homework. I would also guide my domestic help to make the kids' favourite dishes! Remote families also require a huge amount of discipline in ensuring a time to connect, with regular holidays, and focus on key hobbies and studies. But it can all only happen if you gear yourself for it.

Staying by myself also opened me up to my own hobbies in London. When I had some time off from work on the weekends, I focused on some designing courses and spent a huge amount of time with my friends, the relationships I treasure till date. My team was my family-away-from-home and they remain my extended family till date.

This experience ended in December, 2011 and helped me grow stronger. At work, I saw history in the making, the experiential learnings I had during this time in London were invaluable and unparalleled. Staying back in London was a defining decision that I look back at very fondly now. I grew as a human being, from a nervous mother to a great juggler. It was a time-period that I worked beyond the boundaries of my defined roles (not that in any role I have felt restricted) as my ownership of what I did multiplied. I worked through multiple restructuring, leadership changes, rebuilding and redesigning organisation and doing everything that was required strategically to move forward. As a team we worked 24x7 but never felt that it was gruelling work as there was a cautious optimism about a future that we were building by turning the ship around. A fond moment was when in 2011, the business received external recognition for the great turnaround. My professional and personal confidence really blossomed, making me a much more content person!

The work I was doing came to a logical conclusion and it was time to pass on the baton to someone else. I did that with due responsibility so the new incumbent could commence. As I reflect back, there were happy moments at work and tough moments at home, but eventually, it all worked out in the end.

Recently, my daughter quizzically asked me why many mothers of her friends do not work. I explained to her that it is a choice a mother makes and being a homemaker is a tough job as well. Some mothers choose to give up careers as they wish to spend more time with their young ones and there is nothing wrong about this if therein lay their happiness. These are individual and personal choices. She replied, ' Mom, thank you for not giving up your work as I would not know how to live with the guilt of you giving up so much for me. I want to learn how you balanced both work and home.' Just her saying this did made me feel that all the troubles that I had undergone were worthwhile. I told her that I did not really balance anything. It all seems to fall into place when you want to make things work. That is the truth. That has been my experience. I was glad my daughter grew up the way she did! Career for her is not a choice, it will be what she wants!

SUMMARY

The world may view you as a capable professional with a potential to be a leader. However, only if you have the will to exploit the potential and the confidence to drive forward, will this transpire into meaningful results at work. Let your capability make not just a few lives shine but many more. Grab every opportunity to make that difference. And once you have decided to make it big, march on.

- Manage that maze: It is imperative to learn how to navigate through organisational politics by keeping sight of your key focus areas or deliverables, reviewing who is supportive or not, what strategy may work with various people, where and how you should deploy the plans. A circle of trust with allies, like-minded people and mentors provides the much-needed support. They are your best reflectors and let you be prepared for any untoward possibility.

- Perception matters: Perceptions are not realities. But people's reactions towards you are driven by how they perceive you and not necessarily who you are! Hence, it is imperative to know what kind of perceptions exist about you or what people think about you, and then be able to manage these thoughts and the individuals, with the right interventions in case there is a gap or any negativity.

- Be authentic about who you are, your values and beliefs are essential. But be flexible with your style to cater to others' needs. You don't need to make everyone happy. Be aware of who is with you and who is not. I have often found myself putting my key stakeholders on a grid of *impact on my work* and need for *quality of relationship*. Clearly the people to focus on are the ones you share a good bond with. It also helps to proactively seek feedback about yourself both formally and informally.

- Pick your battles: Taking on multiple conflicts does not help and diffuses your energy. So it is best to decide which are the key and high-impact battles to pick and then strategise on the way forward towards achieving the right outcomes. Any conflict takes energy, time and effort to resolve, so one must be sure it is worth the trouble and is being taken on for the right reason and hopefully for the larger good. In such situations, it helps to keep the big picture in mind. Keep an objective outlook and inculcate the ability to zoom in and out to know what a situation entails.

- Speak up: Expressing your thoughts and communicating in larger forums and meetings is important. You need to speak up even if the room is full of all baritones. You don't have to be loud and abrasive, but firm, crisp and clear in your communication. If you don't speak for what you need or deserve, then you will not be heard, and if you are not heard then you don't really exist.

- The juggling act: Being a working mother and straddling two worlds is not easy, but not impossible either. There will be good and bad days at both work and home. Set realistic milestones and then get all the support that you can from family. Be candid in asking for any flexibility at work while keeping up with your work commitments. Also, let go of your guilt and fears that your children need your physical presence all the time. Letting go of this will permit you to leverage other support systems and family members to contribute with what they bring best to the upbringing of your children. Believe in it and you can, you will make it happen! Every cloud has a silver lining! At difficult moments keep in mind, 'This too shall pass'.

6 CONNECT

is the glue that helps build
your impact for all that you
want or need

CONNECT

'Eventually everything connects – people, ideas, objects. The quality of the connections is the key to quality per se.'
– Charles Eames

I understood this much later that life becomes more fulfilling when you start to reflect, consolidate and build on the experience gained during your journey. The game changes when you start to get ready for the race for a leadership position. It is no more about how well you do your day job, That is simply assumed. As you season with experience, a certain level of substance and capability is understood, given you may have already been tested and assessed through various assignments for performance and potential. Now it is all about how you manage the environment, ambiguity of leadership, build the connects and are able to look into the crystal ball to decipher the future. Intuition becomes crucial as you go up the ladder to have it all.

I believe that our ability to connect with others in our environment, allows us to improve our judgement by broadening our thinking while garnering support. Pieces of knowledge, information, or context, in isolation do not serve much purpose at leadership levels. It is the ability to weave these together meaningfully that lends leadership its substance and a sound intuitive decision making.

In my observations, as women grow through this journey, they tend to focus a lot on building their content expertise. They may want to however, leverage their natural relationship strengths more, to nurture connects at various levels: within their teams, peers and seniors in the organisation. Further, as they grow into more senior roles, internal networks may not be sufficient to achieve all that you need to achieve in your role. External networks, awareness of what is going on in the environment can become critical differentiators. Building and nurturing these, however, take concerted time and effort. Nothing worthwhile comes easy! Any professional would do well to systematically evaluate their need for such connections and then work on widening or deepening it, as the need may be. This will help broaden the perspective and your skills, thereby fueling your success.

THE UNDENIABLE POWER OF NETWORKING

I grew up thinking that people at work fall into two categories where either they were my friends, or were not my friends. There was nothing in between. For friends, I had a lot of time and commitment, and I expected the same to be reciprocated. Over a period of two decades of work, I have come to learn, that there are varying shades of friendships and acquaintances. We should not expect or give ourselves completely to each close working relationship. I know this may seem obvious to many but it wasn't to me. Many a time, this led to some painful interaction when there were expectation mismatches.

This changed perspective has been the foundation for me to build my network. I have a core group at work and outside work who I trust completely and engage regularly (and vice-versa), irrespective of roles, transitions and issues. They make my anchor group, as I referred to earlier.

The next critical part of our connect is the broader internal network that is slightly distant but needs to be engaged with periodically. It is important to know people internally (especially in a matrixed environment) as people will associate and work with you effectively only if they have some familiarity with you. The better you know each other, the smoother the working relationship becomes, across business and product silos, enhancing productivity at all ends. However, building these connects and keeping them going, takes effort. You have to constantly find the opportunities at work to connect with people you need to or want to. Building your network is essential for navigating within your operating environment. Women Networks in many organsiations can provide the needed support to women who wish to reach out. Often women lag behind in proactive networking at work due to demands at home after work.

Being an introvert, I used to be hesitant in socialising at work, especially when required to connect at senior levels. Maybe seniority was intimidating as well. I have to confess, this is where I learnt from younger talent who were more confident than I was in getting their share of time with the seniors in the organisation.

I recall, once a junior banker came to meet me in my office in London. He was very excited about his first trip to the New York office and wanted to know what was the best way to reach out to the Global Head of a business. I was taken aback and asked him why he would want to meet him and why he thought the senior would even entertain him? He said that he wanted to connect with him, to ensure that the senior knew who he was (and probably what a great talent he was!). He thought the senior would want to see him if he is one of the few who had the courage to send him an e-mail and ask him for his view about his portfolio and so on. He left me a bit stunned. I figured that he was right. Why had I not thought like this before? Rest assured, he got his time with the Global Head and leveraged that time well to leave some good impressions.

When I did start to proactively reach out to people they were more welcoming than I had expected. When I asked for guidance they willingly offered; when I requested someone to mentor me, to my surprise they gladly consented, even stating that it was their pleasure! Very often, we impose limitations on ourselves about whom and how we should build our network. But there are actually no constraints. Having a good internal network also aids our work, helping with an easier execution of priorities, especially some that require support from a larger group and team. When we work with people across borders, sometimes without ever meeting them, a personal touch can do magic to a working relationship. Without that level of connection, the work, however important it may be, remains transactional.

I required some support to work through a key project that was percieved by the larger team beyond my capabilities. To build their confidence, it was imperative to build an anchor group for support. This required investing in a few peer relationships, which were with both men and women. There were a few people who were similar to me or understood me better than others. I engaged with them proactively as we planned the project. I reached out to few team members and seniors and requested for guidance/ mentoring. Mentors were like mirrors and reflected to me what was going on around me especially if I took a mis-step. Peers and team members helped me align strategies to the larger goal and defended me at appropriate moments in case issues surfaced. We all need some support as none of us are invincible. This anchor group is something I have since then always relied on. The members may change as you change roles. Older members have always remained my friends. As you grow, this group grows along, giving you more strength. You just need to have the motivation to reach out to people!

CONNECTIONS HELP DEAL WITH TRANSITION AND AMBIGUITY

I remember when I had indicated my interest in the India CHRO role, (partly driven by my motivation to come back to India as my husband had been there for a while then), the slate had some very capable candidates. India is considered to be a large and complex role, with a dynamic, everchanging and a somewhat challenging business environment relative to other countries. In addition to this, the management team at that time was being re-organised and had many new members hence leadership development was a key focus. Also, the gender diversity ratio was not where the firm would have aspired for it to be.

Due to various reasons, the job posting had taken time and the process was some time away. I was offered an interim role to move to India that was much smaller than what I was doing in Europe. It probably was at a similar level and scope as my past roles in India. It felt like it was a step back at that time relative to my aspirations. I felt a sense of dissonance during that period. I felt unsure of where I was going with this change. Some of my peers advised me not to move ahead, while my mentors, who probably had a broader perspective, encouraged me to take a leap of faith and helped me deal with the anxiety of ambiguity.

Given my aspirations, I wanted to move up on the next step of the ladder. I was advised that it would be helpful for me to get there and understand the environemnt before the role opened up, even though there was no guarantee of me getting it. If I did not get the role after this interim position, it would have been a setback to my designated path.

One night, I pondered on this transition for a few hours. I reflected back over my investment and effort at work, staying away from family to support the business, in Europe. I started to feel bogged down. Confused with my own feelings and thoughts, I called a senior leader in the bank whom I respected a lot. He was very patient and heard me out. He listened to everything and then said, 'Anu, you need to get there. I am sure you will make this work. If for any reason something does not work out, we will figure this out together. It will be fine.' He also helped me arrive at a Plan B. That was very reassuring and calming.

My conversation with him gave me the strength to battle my anxieties. Even though the situation had not changed, someone underwriting my ambiguity gave me the force to take the leap with a positive mindset and energy. I took the risk of the smaller role and went to India a few months ahead of the role being open. Had I not connected with this mentor, I would probably have not put myself in the reckoning for the job.

I underwent the selection process when the role opened up, in a fearless way and things went in the right direction. I believe that one of the key differentiators I possessed in comparison to the other candidates was that even though I had been away from India for long, my relationships with the relevant stakeholders and business communities were alive. A long-term focused approach to connect turned out to be a big advantage in positioning me well for a large leadership role in India, the first to be done by a woman!

The anxiety I experienced was natural but at times it filled me with some self-doubts. What gave me comfort was having a Plan B, relying upon a senior mentor to remind me that it existed. I could have had my Plan B within the organisation or outside. Going forward, during transitions, I now weigh my options and think through various scenarios, especially when certain variables may be beyond my control. Thinking of the worst that can happen, gives me the much-needed strength to take battles on. My own experience was that I played too safe earlier, sometimes unnecessarily. Usually, we like to have all the steps sorted upfront and want to feel fully equipped to manage the next assignment. Howeer, I learnt that this is not always possible. Insisting on it creates anxiety, hindrances and distances us from our real goals. In life you need to apprehend the future, hoping for the best but being prepared for the worst. Learn to deal with ambiguity, life is ever-evolving and always changing. Believe in yourself, take a bet on yourself. If *you* don't then who else will?

SEEING THE BIG PICTURE TO UNDERSTAND WHO TO CONNECT WITH

As one moves to senior-leadership roles, the environment gets more cloudy and fuzzy. It becomes extremely important to interpret your surroundings correctly to be able to find the right path. Without deciphering your path, it is difficult to continue on the journey and respond to twists and turns around you. As you may have picked up from my earlier experiences, success finally became a result of how I responded to what was happening around me. My misses were also attributable to not reading the tea leaves properly and in time. I had only myself to blame for this. When I stayed back in London, in spite of a personal hardship, it helped me tremendously later in my career. My focus at that time was what I could take away from this experience. I had to keep the bigger picture and a mid-long-term play in mind. It is usually the understanding of this larger picture in the present and the future that helps us connect the dots and take the right decisions. Taking a broader view also helps you zoom in and out of a situation. Very often, while dealing with tricky problems at work, I often zoom myself out of it and look at all that is happening around me – the various players, different processes and then look at how this problem fits in there. This has always helped me find the right way forward. I am then able to see the connection between different issues, dynamics, people and then the decision becomes evident.

I took over the India CHRO role amongst a fairly-new leadership team, a business transitioning out of immense change. In my function, I had inherited a team that was probably yet stabilising itself amidst all this change as well. My first focus was to get the team sorted as without doing so the delivery for the business was almost impossible. Team satisfaction scores had not moved beyond mid-levels over the last few years. The team was a bit fragmented. Most members felt far closer association with people outside their team and stakeholders, rather than being part of an integrated function. My predecessor had actually really helped by infusing some great talent, but he had not been here long enough to do any further. It required a build-up. Some people really did not believe that there would be a positive change. Cynicism was rife.

In the first few weeks, I zoomed out of the situation and almost floated over various issues, teams, sub-teams, got to talking to people, travelling, and understanding what was going on. What was evident was that there was a lot to be done. I commenced by focusing on building a deep connect within the team itself to start with. I also reached out to several key HR stakeholders, search firms and forum chairs to get their objective view of what was needed to be our priorities. This went on to play a key role in the transformation that the team really needed. I do believe that it benefitted not just the team collectively but several individuals tremendously to develop a better perspective, thus allowing us to make a much larger impact for our stakeholders. Over a period of time we organised ourselves differently to internal and external environment. We upgraded ourselves to align to business demands and eventually got on the progressive path where our senior leaders had wanted us to be.

FOCUS ON OUTSIDE – IN VIEW

As is often talked about in the leadership journey that having a view or a perspective from the outside-in is key to understand how external world impacts you or your deliverables. It is extremely important to have an external network to gauge this. To enable this, you have to be constantly connected to the market to understand trends, strategies, bench-marking capabilities, team performance and perceptions about the organisation. There is a wealth of knowledge which is created every day in the market.

Any gap here would imply you will be left behind. Networking with clients, partners, and forums is a great way of getting market intelligence to make you work better and help you march on the path to establish your brand.

One of my earlier managers once told me that Citi was a great platform but you need to build your own leadership brand within that umbrella. That would help you and Citi propel forward! This has always stayed with me. Having a brand, a statement of your purpose and vision also enhances your self-image. It helps your workplace too. However, it also provides a distinct edge about recognition of your capabilities as a professional.

It is important to plan your moves and ensure that you have the right platforms to build your profile. Building your profile is a bit like nurturing a plant with the right soil, fodder and nutrients. Working in New York and London and observing seniors I learnt how effective they were at building connections and relationships. It was meticulous planning that went into it, deciding which people to connect with at work and outside work, decoding messages, and assessing where one wanted to take such a professional relationship to and to which extent it would remain mutual.

In February, 2012, I was quite happy being appointed as the Chief HR Officer for the country. Soon after, I got invited to a Senior HR forum in the country. I felt curious and agreed to attend it as my predecessor and team had attended the same earlier and thought well of it. I did some due diligence with other HR heads and receievd positive references about these meetings.

So I went ahead to attend the forum. There were about a hundred people in the audience, and a panel discussion with some HR seniors was to commence. I met some old friends and made some polite conversation, then grabbed a coffee and a cookie and rushed in to get the right table. The panel discussion started and there were some wonderful thoughts shared by the speakers. As I heard them attentively, it gradually dawned on me that we did all of this work and probably better and more at Citi. Then why were we not talking about it? Why was I there? No one knew me! It was a true moment of reckoning. I returned to the office, having enjoyed the networking, but a bit confused about what I was doing there listening to something I knew already and not talking about what we do well that would benefit the community. From there on, I decided that for most of these forums, my team would represent Citi at the stage. Therein started the journey to build the leadership brand for the team. Some key steps that worked for us were:

Purpose – messaging: This is key and linked intrinsically to what the company, function and your leadership brand is about. Best if this is all aligned….it all comes down to who you are, what your drivers are and what message you want people to take away. We worked on the HR brand, highlighting our mission consistently and reinforcing it through some really good work being done in-house.

Personally, it was about the focus on the value-add which has been a driver throughout my career. It was all about being explicit here.

Think through and be clear about what have been the achievements, what was done well and how one could help the broader fraternity in the market with one's contribution. It is important that people internally and externally perceive the same purpose consistently. Any gaps here will impact the credibility.

Positioning – Place yourself rightly: To maximise the impact, you need to focus on the right people, forums, seminars and networks that help you align with the larger purpose. How you are positioned vis-à-vis your peers impacts how people view you. It is wise to prioritise the key areas (aligned to your needs and messaging), that you need to build your network in, especially since we have limited time in the day to do this. It is important to decide your engagement model – *who* to engage with and *how,* needs to be thought through. There are many social networks in the market, pick a few that could work for you and try to cultivate the depth in the same. Internally, I would recommend having connections with seniors within the country or overseas as appropriate. Reach out to them if they don't know you (how else would they otherwise!) and if they do, deepen that relationship through regular engagements like regular meetings or calls. I find it very effective to reach out to a few seniors when I am dealing with some diverse projects and need some views. That makes people feel included and deepens the connect even further. Skip levels are important to do with seniors when appropriate. Your positioning is key to how people view you externally and internally. Your network, if appropriate, provides you the strength, sponsorship and credibility.

Reach outs: Once you have the purpose and positioning sorted, you have to focus on channels that you will be using to reach out.

When I returned to India, I commenced on a recce across Citi locations with my team. During the course of my settling back, I sought feedback about what the team thought we were doing well. Almost the entire team individually spoke to me about many initiatives which they had worked on and that they felt proud of. My next question was which of these processes or initiatives would be sought as best in the market. The answer to this question was less definitive and more confusing. Most people felt they were doing a great job but were unsure of how good it was, relative to the market and that was surprising. I suspected most people did not even know what the market benchmarks were, leave alone if we were better or worse than that. Therein started the journey of the HR team of India to get more connected to the external world as it continued to focus its efforts internally.

We started to network further with various HR seniors in the market, went to various HR forums, exchanged ideas, and did work pro-bono. We tapped college and school friends in the fraternity and widened the net of HR connectivity. As a team, when we widened our net, we also realised that there were things we were doing well in Citi, and there were some best practices we could learn and leverage from other players in the market. It was a humbling and learning experience. As one participated more and became part of the external network, the more it grew. I got pulled into various initiatives, some even for non-profit and social causes. Citi provided me with a great platform to get into various business-chamber forums like CII, FICCI or ASSOCHAM Easily. Once there, one had to leverage the opportunities to make a bigger impact on behalf of Citi. I realised a lot of the groups were hungry for ideas and commitment to lead these ideas into execution. We undertook some of these initiatives that helped the team, the larger HR fraternity and myself. Over a period of time, this was tremendously helpful in how we navigated the external environment. Also, it strengthened our position as an employer with some great HR practices in the market that gave us well-regarded accolades that made the team feel proud and motivated.

Engagement with appropriate forums build your personal profile too. So long as you don't deviate from the purpose, it adds to the momentum that takes you further in your career.

Market interactions…you represent the brand in whatever you do! This is critical to what and how you learn and renew yourself. It is also what you owe to the organisations you work for. Very often, I would reach out to search firms to get feedback about how the bank was doing, how the market was talking about us and any feedback they would have for us. The market is also very perception-driven. The search firms are very helpful channels to feel the pulse of what may be going on out there. You may choose to collect the feedback and then decide to act on what you feel is credible. Share your experience through knowledge forums and conferences with the larger population.

The more you give, the more you get back. Many a time, when I was in a speaker forum, I have been accosted by many youngsters who seemed starry-eyed, hungry to learn and raring to go. That energy was infectious and I carried that back to my work. One advice I generally give is that when networking externally, try to broaden yourself beyond your functional or technical expertise to enhance your learning. Often you would be called in to share the expertise, but you also carry the brand with you and hence you should be fully ready to engage in discussion beyond your comfort zone.

Once I was in an Industry Confederation panel discussion on leadership, with more than six hundred people in the audience. There was an extensive discussion on HR strategies on how to develop the future leadership. The session was opened to the audience for further queries or questions. If there was an award for the recipient of maximum number of not so happy questions, I would have earned it hands down!. It started with one member of the audience getting up and stating that it is all good to talk about leadership but he felt that was insufficient given his recent poor service experience in one of our branches. He demanded an explanation from me as a representative of Citi. Another kinder soul had a credit card issue. The moderator realised that this interaction may not be going in the desired direction and tried interjecting. However, in front of a large audience it was important that I stepped up and answered these questions on behalf of the Bank. I requested the moderator to step back. I pacified those members of the audience by empathising with their issues and assured them of our process of continuous improvement wherein each relationship manager is expected to be a leader in solving customer-service issues. That is the ethos which we encouraged and we may not be perfect, but strive to be! This did satisfy those individuals and we got the discussion back on track. Reflecting back, if I had not answered the question, I would have not only had a more irate client but may have also had an unfinished message of customer-fulfilment promise that Citi holds.

When you are talking externally, think on your feet and be ready to take any interaction in your stride keeping your authenticity. My experience has been that people bond with honesty! The incidental fallout of all of this is that it builds your profile holistically and keeps you better connected. This will always be helpful if you were to review options in your career journey as well.

Media is a great platform and it is important to engage with the appropriate agencies on behalf of the organisation. My experience has taught me that right channels, and a genuine, authentic relationship helps here. In the past, we have reached out to the media to make them aware about what we do in Citi and in HR which they were not fully aware of. In such interactions, there was so much that I learnt from them about market practices that I had been able to replicate in Citi. Fortunately, I have had no bad experiences here and have been able to leverage some senior people in the media as sounding boards for thought leadership. The breadth and depth of the feedback has left me impressed. Openness is usually reciprocated.

Social media is gaining prominence for intercations and communications across various segments of the population. It is a medium which has gained such a high momentum over the last few years that not being a part of it may actually pull one back. Given the viral nature of the medium, it has a tremendous reach that can be leveraged to have your message delivered broadly. Start a blog, tweet regularly, get on Tumblr, Facebook, LinkedIn, the list is endless. Working in companies like ours, these engagements have to be treated with caution as very often you do not just represent yourself but also the company brand you work for. Win–win is to focus on topics and trends that help the company and also the message that one wants to disseminate. I have been a beneficiary of a lot of knowledge from following various people and networks on these sites. Tumblr was a revelation to me about how teenagers work and think today, their likes and dislikes. Given most people on Tumblr do not operate with their real names, they tend to be more forthcoming about their views. Blogging is very helpful to gain perspective on certain thoughts and also for sharing your ideas. I find that people on social media, are usually willing, appreciative, critical and encouraging at the same time. My challenge sometimes has been dealing with issues on social media that are generic and company-related and people start to treat me as a spokesperson for the company, which I am, but may not always be authorised to respond to them.

Alumni networks: When I came back to India, business was faced with a lot of change that led to a lot of uncertainty. To get a sense of the past events and present perceptions, I reached out to the alumni network to understand what was going on in the market and how they saw us from an external perspective. All of them were very welcoming and encouraged me on the road ahead. Most of them connected almost immediately and it felt like meeting family members of a larger group. The language, the ethos, time together – these bonds had stood the test of time. We had a lot in common, which could never be taken away, irrespective of where we worked then. I believe people may move on from the organisation but they continue to identify themselves in someways with the brand. There is collegial glue which keeps the alumni together. Alumni networks can be very strong proponents and partners, according to my experience. During these interactions, I gathered feedback, thoughts and understood their views on a range of subjects, sought their advice about various topics and they helped me with ideas to strengthen the message and the brand across sectors and the industry. It is a special group for me and I am sure that I will always stay in touch with them.

Speaker Forums are great to network and also very helpful for disseminating your message. Media has a broader impact,

However, forums helped up provide the depth of our messages within a certain community. Chairing a few forums, being a part of thought leadership, building through speaker series or exchange of ideas through panel discussions are a great way to reach out to the external world with your message. I have truly enjoyed this and have tried to share and exchange my thoughts in the most earnest way.

Perspective and community building: As I gained from all the interactions in forums, media and alumni, I decided to also give back to the fraternity and the industry at large. It was about being useful and supportive to others in the same way as someone had helped me. I started mentoring a few upcoming, talented individuals in various universities, engaged in pro-bono coaching of people outside my organisation. We also worked on various summits to create some knowledge platforms for younger talent who could learn and leverage the experience and learnings of others. I worked on some research papers with the campuses and did sessions with students. Also, I undertook some CSR work with my team to contribute to society at large. I spent time with an NGO for children. These experiences made me truly humble and I realised how privileged one had been when I witnessed the real agony of the parents and understood how the lovely, innocent smiles of such lively, suffering children gave those parents the courage to face everything. Any education, skill, and moral support that we could provide to the family was extremely fulfilling. Across all these activities, the more we gave, the more one got back in terms of learning about life. Contributing towards building perspectives and knowledge of others, truly moulded me up to be a better human being, thereby making me a better professional.

Finally, building a profile is about making your statement and communicating with the larger environment about who you are and what you stand for. This helps to establish your relationships with a larger community beyond your immediate work. Given the multiple priorities faced at senior levels, most women tend to be more consumed at work or home and seem to miss giving this aspect of their leadership journey due importance. The ones who do gain from the outcome of this investment can vouch for its magic. As I engaged with the above activities, I missed having more women in forums or networks. Some who were there were very good at keeping the connection going after the initial meetings which was tremendously helpful in deepening the relationship for the future. I really respect them for the continuous efforts and have embedded that in my own efforts towards building relationships. These women also became a great support for women networks and community in due course of time.

SUMMARY

Having the right connects makes all the difference in creating the bigger picture and then adding colour to it. Mitch Albom has rightly said, 'There are no random acts...We are all connected... You can no more separate one life from another than you can separate a breeze from the wind...'

- There are various milestones that you need to cross to establish an identity that is *you*. This is done by defining your leadership brand that defines *you* and making that known. This needs to be aligned to your purpose, values and the bigger picture that you have painted for yourself.
- Networking or building connections is critical for a variety of reasons: you need friends who understand you and can be a pillar of support in times of difficulty. You need mentors who value you and can be a source of guidance in times of ambiguity, you need seniors and leaders who see potential in your work, purpose and can help you reach out to a wider audience. You need to remain relevant in the ever-changing work context.
- Leverage media, forums, social media and alumni. In fact, with the world becoming smaller with an ever-increasing focus on social media, the speed and extent of your connections with the right people greatly influences the speed of your success.
- Women often underplay these connects due to hesitation to reach out or pressure of familial responsibilities. However, with some effort, planning, prioritisation and effective management, they can build these connects. Remaining honest to the relationship is the cardinal rule to the success of any relationship.

Your network is your safety trampoline that will never let you fall and even if you do, it bounces you right back with force!

7 COLLABORATION, PARTNERSHIP AND... COMPETITION

extend your hand to get
someone else's

COLLABORATION, PARTNERSHIP AND... COMPETITION

'Alone we can do so little; together we can do so much'
– Helen Keller

Collaboration fosters a spirit of common purpose. In this spirit, people work together to realise common goals. To have collective success at work, our efforts need be focused on contributing towards one another's success by giving each other the required support. Partnership with key individuals and fostering these relationships is a part of a successful career journey. Women need to actively solicit this support and proactively engage with key players and not be passive, waiting for help to come by. In my experience, men can often be great mentors and can support women to navigate the workplace.

Any career journey cannot be traversed alone. Each one of us needs the help of our ecosystem to thrive and succeed. It is essential for us to keep nurturing this ecosystem. Along my journey, I have realised the tremendous value of this ecosystem, without which it would not have been possible to cover the distance that I have, professionally or personally. Right behaviours and attitudes are essential. At various points in time, one relied on various stakeholders, managers, peers, teams and partners to provide one with a spectrum of support: assistance on the job, guidance, direction, someone to share personal responsibilities with or simply a listening ear.

A LOT DEPENDS ON YOUR BEHAVIOURS AND ATTITUDE

'You have to accept that you will never be good enough for some people, no matter how hard you try. Now whether that is going to be their problem or yours is up to you' – Bryant Mcgill

This quote is very close to my heart. It will help you too, to decide your reactions to certain people depending on how vested you are in them. Your value does not change because of someone's ability or inability to see your worth. In my career journey there have been highs and lows, successes and failures. However, my will to continue on the path was primarily driven by how I viewed these events.

One of my key mantras has been to keep an optimistic and hopeful attitude no matter which problem pulls me down, at home or work, and there have been plenty of them! I might have had my moments, but I have learnt to bounce back in minutes, hours or a few days. Earlier, I attempted to do everything well, to the point of perfection, which in reality was impossible. This used to lead to frustration that would make me negative and pessimistic at times. Then, it would be a downhill journey from thereon, impacting my disposition at work and home. Gradually, I started to reconcile to the fact that I could manage only so much and sometimes some things *would* go wrong and that was *okay*. However, in the long run, I believed that it would work out. That instilled in me hope, and a positive attitude that infused much-needed energy to deal with issues constructively. A positive and realistic attitude is imperative for you to set the right tone with your professional and personal relationships. It also helped me be less emotive and personal with issues, reducing the negative intensity in general. When I was undergoing transition coaching and I received 360-degree feedback, and my first reaction was of denial of the not so positive aspects of the feedback. My coach pushed me to get more objective in order to deal with what was needed for appropriate action planning results.

Most women deal with multiple stresses and multi-task all the time between personal and professional priorities – an optimistic outlook defines how you will respond to problems faced along the way.

Our behaviour is fundamental to how people experience us, understand us and collaborate with us. At each progressive rung of the ladder we require different behaviours and responses to situations. Earlier in our career, when most of us are managing ourselves, focused on goals or the task at hand, our priority is mostly delivery of work. As we season and become senior, we start focusing on a blend of getting the work done through a team while managing the leadership team above us in the pyramid. If successful, we finally transition to being a senior leader managing a franchise or a function. In my experience, these crossroads or transitions are understood intellectually but executing the change in behaviour is not always as easy. Change in management style with team and peers is critical.

The *power play* needs to be understood as one graduates towards the next innings of the leadership journey. I found that my recent leadership inning was the toughest; as it demanded a very different behaviour from how I had worked thus far. Some behaviours that required changes – were being empathetic yet assertive (not aggressive) in communication, being more vocal yet listening more all the time, learning to exert your power subtly or directly but yet keeping the compassion, letting go of control and trusting the team on delivery, while not shirking your accountability. This fostered a spirit of camaraderie as our dependancies grew on each other. As I grew into leadership roles, I had to learn to leverage a consensus approach on decision-making in the diverse environment we worked to foster collaboration. But as expected, I had to also ensure that the goals were met by being in charge, if there was a crisis. Different situations require different behaviours and style. My view is that this flexibility of style can be easily imbibed by women given they are so much more used to handling multiple and conflicting demands between home and work ! It is about being self aware.

Flexing your style and understanding the appropriate behaviours that foster collaboration and empathy, is the key to getting support from your team and stakeholders. Many a time this becomes a process of learning and unlearning. As I grew into bigger roles, the expectations changed not just from my managers and stakeholders, but also from peers and team members. It was my privilege to lead people and I had to step upto it, by listening to them, supporting them and also challenging them. One of my recent managers once told me that people expect to be led well. This was true as leadership is a responsibility not an entitlement. Depending on the team members, their collective temperament and prevailing culture of the groups, there may be subtle practices and norms which have to be understood and integrated with. As a new leader even if you want to change the culture, it is imperative to understand these unsaid rules and be a part of the team bonds to bring about the spirit of collaboration.

MANAGERS

Managers are a product of what they have managed in the past. To have a collaborative relationship you need to understand them and you have to ensure they understand you! During the course of my career, I have had some great managers who also mentored me, while some who probably needed more mentoring themselves. At leadership levels, you may consider choosing your managers as much as the role if you can, as your success is integrally tied to how this relationship works out. Someone once told me, 'you are as good as your manager thinks you are. If he or she thinks you are not doing well, then go work for another manager!'

Having worked with quite a few managers, both men and women, I felt that once a working relationship was formed, one had to go through a bit of an education process with them, especially the male managers, about how I worked, my drivers and expectations. Sometimes their management style was driven by what they had experienced in the past with women subordinates, or by their lack of experience with them. At times, it was also driven by their personal outlook about women based on their socialisation and what they may have observed at home or college.

All in all, you need to help yourself by helping them understand who you are and what collaboration you want/need from them to help your career. This dawned on me even more clearly, when I decided to work between cities or countries at different points of time in my career. It was not only a different way for me to manage my work, but also a learning experience for my managers who had never had a chaotic woman employee like me working all over the place! They had to come up the learning curve as well and had changed their work habits to accommodate this new work practice in their life. And they did support me once they understood how committed I was, irrespective of how and where I worked from. It took some candid conversations to set some realistic expectations and patience at both ends to get used to this way of working. Finally the real deal is in how your perform and deliver!

There are various views about how it is to work for a woman manager. I have had one talented, woman manager in my career (there are very few on the top!), whose style was slightly different than mine, in terms of how she engaged with the team. She was much focused on work and very efficient with her time. She was hard-working and always on top of the game. I experienced that same commitment and drive on work from her as I did with the male managers. Contrary to prevaling perceptions, I had more baby talk and family chats with men than women managers who were more focused on getting the work done on time so that they could retrun home timely to attend to their family responsibilities!

At senior levels, most of us need a sense of confidence and trust in our leadership. That usually inspires a leader to lead better. Working in Europe or in the US, exposed me to different styles of leadership, working styles and ways of communication. Gender or culture was less relevant once the leaders set a common purpose and credibly backed the team to deliver it. All managers have some learning to offer. We can often learn by emulating their strengths and also by ensuring that we don't make their development areas our own! Working with tough managers or those we don't generally relate to, provides a different kind of learning about what not to do.

TEAMS

It is critical to empower people along the way so they beocome your collaborative partners. A strong team is a reflection of a leader's strength. The stronger one's team is, the more one is able to achieve. A leader's success is not measured by what he or she has been able to accomplish alone, but by his/her ability to identify talent, nurture teams and drive them to excel. In order to achieve more, it is essential to keep building collaborative self-reliant teams. The more leaders do this, the more people want to work with them, leading to greater achievement. It is also essential to have a flexible style, adapting to the needs and development of varying team members. Women managers are naturally well-equipped with many of such softer skills to nurture others. These are core for managing a team well. I have seen both men and women leaders do well here.

Diverse teams provide different perspectives and solutions for problem solving. Such groups collaborate well to challenges with creative problem solving. There is a lot of debate about fostering more gender diversity in teams. I have had most of my experience in the HR function. This function somehow has had a higher number of women. Many a time I felt the function needs to have a better balance of men and women. The driver for this imbalance may be due to the fact that HR is perceived to be an internal support function, more intuitive with softer skills at the core, less high-pressure and may be more flexible. Reality can't be farther away from this. On numerous occasions, across all my HR roles, the complexities that I have had to manage, have been beyond a lot of line managers' comprehension, the stress or pressure one has undergone have been similar to sales pressure, the risk I have had to tread, put me on the line like any other.

Having a balanced number of men and women in the team is important. In my experience I have found men in HR are very intuitive and adept at soft skills apart from having a great potential to multi-task. I have found that male team members have been fairly empathetic as required by the function. Also I have found when men in the team and peer group are engaged with the diversity agenda, the likelihood of its success is very high. They promote the inclusive approach, propagate sensitisation and help us work through the unconscious biases at work. Different perspectives foster innovation and a collaborative spirit of learning together.

PEERS AND STAKEHOLDERS: COLLABORATION OR COMPETITION!

For anyone climbing up the ladder, the competition is rife across all levels and at each step you take. As you move forward, you realise that for any leadership role, it is the survival of the fittest. Usually after decades of experience you are yet in the race, because you are good at what you do and how you do it. You have cracked the code. From here to the C-Suite role, things get more exciting. It is no more about how well you did in the past but how you step up your game going forward, how you size up the environment and flex your style to respond to it. What has made you successful till now may not necessarily make you successful in the future, unless you understand this. Peers are collaborators but can also be competition, so these relationships may change and need to be managed sensitively. Women often get caught up between relationships at this juncture when objectivity and keeping an eye on the goal is necessary.

At senior levels neither is everyone a friend, nor a foe. Pick the ones you can trust. You do compete amongst friends and rivals both. For women, I have seen that this results in their competitors underplaying their strengths and maybe overplaying issues. Women need to step up the game here. People may throw many things at you, including gender stereotypes, if that helps their agenda. In the past as I progressed to senior roles, some of the comments I learnt to ignore were, 'Can you really manage these dynamic bankers and their style?' Or, 'Can you manage tricky union issues?' I never understood why these questions were asked of me. Was it my competence level or my gender? Questions seemed to imply that I was too soft to handle this.

During my career transitions, I learnt that peer relationships that are managed well through continuous engagement, can foster collaboration that will help achieve success. Peers and key stakeholders can be helpful and constructive support if we have some common ground and sometimes common foes! Also, this relationship needs to be nurtured at both ends. It is not right to expect co-workers to collaborate with us if we are not able to add value in return. Offering our own support, inputs and genuine interest in their pursuits, allows us to build a symbiotic network of colleagues – peers, stakeholders and seniors.

We are aware that many leadership or management teams are yet to bring about a balance in styles with more women at the table. This poses a unique challenge for a few (sometimes a bit lonely !), senior women who are there. How they flex their style or adopt appropriate behaviours to influence and make an impact in the senior forums, is key to how the tone is set for other women entering senior management teams. I don't wish to generalise, but in my career I have witnessed two reactions from women in such situations, though there could be a third one which is somewhere between the two.

– Some senior women debate the appropriate style to manage the male-dominated board room but fall back into a comfort zone by being the *calm and nurturing* team member. This is usually less effective. In order to make peace, women step back and play a passive role or at best a facilitator's role in such senior meetings. Either ways they are unable to be decision-makers. In such cases, women are essentially working within a stereotype that is self re-inforced. It sometimes emanates from the need to be accepted by being what a woman is expected to be within the social norms which creates no dissonance and keeps harmony. Standing out of the normal can be intimidating and uncomfortable for this group. They tend to sit back from key debates as it involves conflicts and generates a lot of negative energy, which is not always easy to handle to keep yourself on track. The relatively aggressive behaviours of men can sometimes intimidate women and they are unable to retort vociferously when they must.

- Some senior women tend to change themselves to be more assertive by either using a firm tone of voice and body language, frequent usage of action words and pushing for decisions. I do feel for these women, having experienced this dilemma myself. It often comes down to balancing between who you really are versus who you need to be to command your position. It is ideal when there is no conflict but it can be tough if the demand of the role and the related style may not be natural. Very often I have witnessed, such tough, assertive women are perceived negatively by their colleagues, both men and women. Assertive women are threatening to the traditional persona of a caring, sacrificing and demure woman. I found that assertive women get branded as bossy, self-centred and political, contrary to a man who may be exhibiting similar behaviours. A man with such a style is perceived far more positively and is understood to be a natural leader. A question it does raise, however, is that does a woman need to behave like a man to get ahead? Maybe, or maybe not. I have also witnessed some of these women leaders who flex their style do make it forward though do not always become part of the "boys' club" and many not feel the need to ! Unfortunately, sometimes the bigger issue for 'aggressive' women is the alienation from the other women who may not relate to this overt ambition or drive. This is why it can get even more lonely at the top for some women.

You may want to think what style you want to leverage. There is nothing right or wrong as both have some benefits and some costs. The question to reflect upon is what sits well with you and what is most effective in the circumstances that you may be in.

I have tried both these styles in various roles in my career. The first one was easy, uncontroversial, collegial and acceptable but is not the leadership play, especially in boards or management teams. The second one is tougher. You don't have to be abrasive but assertive and must have the right intent. In this case, the mould has to be broken and hence, there can be negative consequences, misperceptions and branding that you may not like. However, the opportunity for you to get to a decision maker's role is possible. Over a period of time you need to build allies and a set of people who understand and appreciate your intent and any negative perceptions may fade away. The issue is that it takes time and one needs to have the conviction to be able to withstand some tough times until then. But then again, a leadership journey is not meant to be easy!

MENTORS

Apart from direct managers, with whom my straight conversations and explicit statement of emotions experienced, helped bridge the gap, I also benefitted from some great mentors and sponsors. I think in a male-dominated world, you have to first understand the rules of the game even before you can think about changing them. These mentors were tremendously supportive. I have made a constant reference to them in my journey. In my experience my mentors who have been men, have helped me interpret and crack the code.

To engage with mentors, you need to gauge your chemistry, mentor profile, impact and reach out to people you feel comfortable with. Ask them to be your mentors. If you don't know them, have a colleague or HR facilitate. Most organisations have mentoring programmes that you could volunteer for. You could also reach out to people outside work.

My mentors have helped me by being explicit and direct (some times much more than my female friends) about what worked or not, what I did well or didn't. This was done in a non-evaluative way and hence it worked. I have some important takeaways as below, from these mentoring sessions.

- Firstly, I learnt that objectivity is a wonderful quality to cultivate especially when you deal with problems. Being objective enables your constructive thinking. Getting it straight was easier to comprehend for me. Most of my male mentors were less emotive about the feedback they gave, especially when I did not get something right
- Secondly, I was taught the value of commitment at work to achieve the larger goals. However, with commitment comes focus, leading to a no-nonsense attitude which I saw more in men than women. I learnt from them the value of being intolerant of bad behaviours, practices or distractions, if I was doing the right thing with a hundred per cent commitment. Work hard and play hard.
- Thirdly, they helped me look at the big picture more clearly. With one of my mentors in New York, I remember being told how I needed to sometimes step outside the bubble at work. This helps to look at interconnections between different parts at work, playing of various interactions and connections between multiple people and departments. I often apply this and it really helps.
- Lastly, I was taught not to underplay myself and be ready to position myself rightly for the appropriate opportunities. Men market themselves better. Women are usually more self-deprecating and look for perfection in most things including themselves. My male mentors always advised me that when you are ready about sixty per cent for the next leap, then jump! You will find yourself growing fast into the next opportunity so long as you are convinced this is the right one for you!

From my experience, I think working with any mentor is helpful. However, I found the experience with men mentors particularly helpful in learning the operating styles on the banking floors, understanding thought processes around the table, and hence I was better prepped for dealing with business problems in a male-dominated environment. All the men who mentored me had seen me at work that mattered to them. They did not mentor me because I struggled at the workplace on the basis of gender!

I remember when I moved into one of my leadership roles overseas; my announcement was to be released to business seniors in a few days. The business heads, who had also been a mentor came forward, and decided that he would induct me in the business by introducing me to all the major stakeholders in person, across the floor rather than sending an e-mail. I was unsure what that meant but went along with him. He took me from one office cabin to another, giving each one a short description of what I was expected to do and how important that was! He did not have to do this. In retrospect, this was a great intervention. His short, but face-to-face introduction, gave me the right positioning that made my transition and induction extremely smooth. It got me at the table right away!

Like other individuals I have had my fair share of low points in my career. Sometimes I felt one worked hard but did not get rewarded enough. At other times, I did not get promoted when I felt deserving of it. I have been a victim of politics and fell flat on my face sometimes, not knowing how to deal with it. Even more difficult times were when I struggled with new managers or was unsure of how to expand my network or circle influence beyond immediate colleagues. In all such situations I benefitted from a lot of support from all my mentors. Their most significant contribution was to help me understand environment, colleagues, managers and peers and giving me the requisite advice to deal with them. Sometimes they stood behind me like a rock when I hit the bottom and ensured I resurrected myself. I would like to acknowledge their contribution and express my heartfelt gratitude to them.

HUSBAND/PARTNER

Having a partner from a similar background, pursuing similar careers, having divergent thoughts at work, but aligned at home was immensely helpful. We understood each other's good days and bad days at work. We made space when one of us was clouded at work and did not complain (or at least not too much!). In my experience, good compatibility at home naturally reflects in your work and transfers the harmony in what each of us does. This truly gave me the wings to soar.

Having an understanding partner or husband, who is willing to give your career due importance, gives you the much-needed momentum. Someone who is willing to share the responsibilities of home and children when you need to travel out at work, is a relief. I have been fortunate in this aspect. Sandeep and I have worked through our relationship with equal importance to each other's career aspirations. He was the reason that I felt strong enough to stay back in London and do what I really wanted to do at work. I recall, when I was confronted to take this decision I was devastated with chaos and confusion. With family relocating back to India (including the children), I was unsure of whether I could really pursue my career interests as it had some hardship built in for family and self. I was overridden with guilt.

At this time it was my husband who stepped in and helped me regain my composure and confidence. At such a juncture, if I did not have his words of encouragement, I may not have taken a leap of faith irrespective of the role and the rewards. After all, it was the first time I was deciding to stay away from the children and that made me nervous and guilty.

Even now I split time between Mumbai and Delhi for work, spending more time in Mumbai while home is in Delhi. We work together on how we manage our domestic affairs amidst both our work and travel, with support from our parents. There have been many moments where I would have slipped at work, if I did not have his support. There were days when the children were unwell, and that is one thing which still drives me insane with anxiety. Sometimes these moments coincided with important meetings in office and I used to get conflicted as the children's well-being came before anything else! That's when his sane advice of keeping calm and his offer of working from home would keep me going. We of course, took turns but the important bit was that *we did take turns* and it was not simply for me to deal with it as a mother. He took equal responsibility for it. We split our time for making for school PTAs and as a thumb rule share summaries from the PTA so the school affairs are not lost on either of us (Sandeep is more prompt on this than I am!). He has an equally demanding role and some times more stressful than mine, with travels across multiple countries but this extra effort to share responsibilities goes a long way in keeping our family and careers on track.

Sandeep has always understood me and let me pursue my career interests in the way that I would like to. We have had some basic family rules. We are together on all weekends and do not do business travel unless very critical. All birthdays and anniversaries are celebrated together and we would travel back if we are away. These are personal and special moments for us as a family. We are together working out of the city at least one week in a month (one weekend to another) and one of us if not both, has to be there for any school event. Life is not perfect and neither are we! Hence we do not kill ourselves if one of us cannot make it for a school show for a valid reason. Our children have grown up to understand this and appreciate our efforts. They understand that we try and that is what matters!

Sandeep and I usually do not take or talk work at home. Well, I am not always as consistent! We both have intense roles and usually we try our best not to carry that stress to our family. It is not usual for us to seek work-related advice from each other as we do distinct things. Hence, neither of us is aware of each other's office dynamics nor do we feel that this should intrude on family time.

Husbands/partners are critical for a woman to be able to pursue her career given all the three crossroads of mobility, marriage and maternity, are faced with your spouse. It is the compatibility between the two, mutual respect and appreciation and empathy that gives the woman her self-confidence to rise above social prejudices, norms and the feeling of how she may be neglecting home by being at work. Trust me, none of this would have been possible if Sandeep had not stood behind me like a firm supporter. It has been collaboration in its truest form, without which it would not have been possible for me to pursue my dreams.

It is essential for women and their partners to work in tandem and provide each other with a true partnership.

MEN AND WOMEN COLLABORATING AT WORK

A difficult issue that often crops up but not discussed explicitly is, how much and how closely should women engage with male colleagues at work. Whilst dealing with peers, sub-ordinates and managers, most women have to balance a thin line between not staying aloof yet not getting too close. Staying slightly further away would keep you away from the action that could be *really* going on among the team members. Many women express their inability to attend social engagements late in the day, evening drinks sessions that could lead to missing out on some critical interactions. These may be critical to be part of the 'group' and decision making that is discussed and executed informally rather than formally.

I have often heard from my women friends that they don't want to go out for drinks or dinner as either they need to be back home on time or that it would be misconstrued. Some women colleagues have talked to me about how they do not feel part of the 'club' because they don't feel comfortable being out with the group late at night. I don't think we should do that if we feel uncomfortable, however nothing is preventing us from having lunch, coffee or an early evening glass of wine if the informal peer networking is important and needed on the job to build certain connections. For some women, staying away from these social interactions is also due to the fear of their character being misjudged in informal interactions. Many women choose to keep their working relationships with male colleagues very distant at work due to this apprehension. This is tricky and will have to be judged on the basis of the male colleague one is dealing with. However we should not generalise this, else, it has the risk of lacking depth and the kind of proximity you may need at work with various colleagues. Also, it could make it difficult to integrate with the larger group of men in the team, leading to some social isolation. It is important to keep a balance in such interactions by being honest to yourself. The lens people see you with is a reflection of their mindset and not a reflection of your character.

Sometimes I have had feedback from women about the language used in certain places. As a part of the work culture in most organisation, no foul language is acceptable and you have to draw the line on what makes you feel uncomfortable and be diplomatically explicit about it. This could also apply to any demeaning behaviour faced. Drawing a line is important because people do need to understand when you mean business.

If you need to professionally bridge a working relationship and have a common goal, how you behave, what you say, matters to how people see you in these interactions. Men and women working closely can sometimes lead to misperception about relationships. This may be attributed to a great working chemistry and may not be an interaction more than what is required to get the work done. Unfortunately when such working chemistry prevails, I have heard more gossip about women than men. It leads to unhealthy chatter which women can find to be more career limiting than men. In certain situations, I have seen the success of a woman was not credited to her good work but to relationships at work. There is no shortcut to success. Working harder and smarter is core. For all the progress in the social outlook about women at work, I have found this one to be the most regressive trend. These misconstrued optics, bother many career women and keeps them away from engaging constructively and freely at times.

I had a friend who was a seasoned professional in an organisation and her job demanded extensive travel on client work. She seemed to successfully juggle her life with priorities at work and at home with two children. Given that she was required to work on a few high impact projects with one of her male colleagues, they were expected to work together and accompany each other for client meetings. Obviously they worked on the deals while travelling and that implied spending a lot of time together. They worked well and both of them were thorough professionals who were very achievement-oriented and driven at work. They shared a good working relationship and were a formidable combination for acquiring client deals.

Unfortunately, during the course of these big projects, their extensive interactions at work started to be noticed by many work colleagues in a light that was unrelated to these projects. It gradually started to generate whispers in the corridors and led to unnecessary gossip at work. Their working chemistry started to be perceived as an unprofessional alliance. Since I knew her well, I was also aware that there was nothing beyond the working relationship here. However I saw my friend being gravely impacted by this at a personal level. She felt extremely demoralised and tainted when she picked up these vibes in office. She struggled with how she should respond to it and started to pull herself out of the projects where this male colleague was engaged. This was neither good for her career as it took her away from the important deals, and nor for the organisation as these two formed a good team. For the fear of being further maligned and suffering from acute anxiety about any reprisal at home from her partner, she eventually left the organisation.

Take a moment to reflect on this incident. Who gained and who lost? I think apart from a set of dysfunctional and stereotypical minds that relished in gossip, all others lost what could have been a great opportunity for them. The male colleague/manager lost a great team member, the woman in question relinquished a great role and an opportunity to make it big. Most importantly, the organisation lost a great employee, a great team chemistry and some great business opportunities. Could this have been prevented? Could this relationship have been viewed more objectively? I don't think there are easy answers and some of these problems relate to a much larger environment and expectations from men and women working together.

Invariably, I have found that women tend to opt out much faster due to the reasons stated in the situation earlier. They feel more vulnerable and are more prone to negative branding in these instances. Some feel that the credit for their success is given to relationships with men who they work with. In certain places, some women have been seen to progress only because of close connectivity with men. Their competence is ignored and this creates a further problem for successful women with self-respect, who would like to be seen as moving forward on the basis of their competence. Women perceive this as a serious reputational damage, and something that has a potential to have long-term negative consequences to their other close relationships at home. However, when I see men in similar situations, my observation has been that they are probably less impacted than women, more so at a personal level. Men clearly do not see many long-term consequences to their personal or professional relationships and seem to keep these two separate. Even if they are a victim of gossip, it may sometimes actually enhance their image at work rather than them being perceived as victims.

These situations are a real dilemma for some women and due to the fear of their interactions being misperceived, tend to withdraw from extensive interactions with men. There are also cultural elements at play here. For instance, certain cultures in Asia or Middle East are more conservative in this aspect, which makes it even tougher for women to engage more with men, at work. There are differing etiquettes about how men and women work together as social interaction norms for women are different depending on geographies.

Unfortunately, these are some grey areas that do not have clear answers and it is essential for male colleagues to be sensitive in such situations. If they are willing to work together to resolve such issues rather than leave their female colleagues to fend off the situation by themselves, it would be a lot easier to put such matters to rest. One does not have any generic advice for this issue apart from sharing that a balance needs to be maintained. Be conscious of the optics around you at workplace. However, don't let unnecessary gossip bother you as there are instances where your competitors will pull you down even if it gets a bit ugly. Deal with it by raising the bar your performance and keeping the momentum at work. Having allies, friends and mentors around to help you with this situation through their constructive moral support. Be a fighter and be true to yourself. Don't let any of this ever break you down. Insecure minds sometimes tend to create such problematic situations. Sometimes there are no remedies for envy. Deal with it with dignity and grace by focusing on doing good work in a smart way. Over time people move on to other topics.

CAN MEN HELP?

There is a lot of debate about how women leaders can be groomed, need for more women required in the C-suite to change the balance of power or bring about a cultural change.

However, the corporate world still remains male-dominated, regardless of this debate that has been carrying out over two decades, though the focus has become more intense lately. In spite of concerted efforts towards awareness and policies we still see very few women making it to leadership roles and even lesser in the C-suite. *Why*?

A significant variable that governs women's ability to reach to the top management is the engagement and support of men. While quite a few corporate men believe that teams with significant numbers of women perform more successfully, fewer recognise the challenges women face. In my experience there are yet some ignorant men who are less likely to comprehend this, due to their socialisation. A few years ago, a sensitisation training had been carried out for a group of seniors in one of organisation that an associate of mine worked with. At the outset, the facilitator asked two key questions that set the tone for sensitivity in the session.

Question one: How many of you have a working wife who is pursuing a professional career like you?

Question two: How many of you have had a working mother who has also pursued her career?

For question one, about four of the forty hands went up in the room and for question two, about two hands shot up. This was quite telling. It struck me that if these men have not had any career women in their life, how will they ever empathise or understand what a career woman goes through? So how do we carry these men on this journey? I have found at work that very often if these men had women team members on maternity leave, after they returned to work, the general assumption made by them was that the new mother may want to take a break or may not want key roles at work. This emanated from how they had seen things at home and maybe experienced a few other women around them. However, in spite of men trying to be helpful by giving returning mothers easier roles to help them (does work for some), they unintentionally created problems for some career women who probably wanted to come back to some serious work or do a key assignment in a flexible way without compromising on delivery. Some of these men needed to be sensitised to the fact that different women/ mothers may look for different ways to bring balance in their work life.

My own experience taught me that men are a critical part of the career journey. I was hired by men, mentored largely by men and progressed with their support. They have a critical role to play at home and at work if you want to fulfil your career aspirations. Women have to also play a part in carrying them along. I worked hard and they reciprocated by investing in my career, supported me in building my experiences that enabled learning. Once they saw me working hard and adding value, I was treated like any other employee who was doing well on his/her job. I had access to all the support or choices of any role that I felt equipped to do. The decision or the risk was mine to take. This probably was easier at junior levels because there was enough space between levels, no liabilities or less responsibilities of family on self and a hunger to prove oneself at work. All I was keen to do was grow, learn and do as many meaningful assignments. I think my own inclination to learn, enabled me to explore and contribute better. This helped me add value through varied assignments at work which garnered a lot of support for me from seniors. Even during various maternity crossroads, so long as I was clear about what I wanted, I was able to express it and get it from my male bosses, who were rather surpirsed that I did not want flexibility when I had a baby! What helped me was being clear about what I wanted at work, where I wanted to go in the medium term and having a credible relationship with stakeholders and managers. As women, very often we look for inclusive culture; however, my own belief is that sometimes embracing the organisational drivers helps to be included.

During my journey, I have had eight male bosses and one female boss. I have enjoyed working with all of them with a few moments of stress thrown in (as with all relationships). While I was in India, I worked with a manager who pushed me into a few stretch assignments. I never felt he differentiated between male or female members in the team when it came to being stretched at work! However, I recall once, when I returned after a family situation, he went easy on some urgent work priorities with me. That was a bit odd and I felt either he was not happy with my work or maybe did not feel confident that I could deliver on those goals, So I had to sit down with him over coffee and explain to him my frustration of feeling light at work. He was taken aback as he thought he was helping me by taking some work away from me. I actually needed my work back to keep me away from domestic stress. Sometimes men have to be educated, especially when they too are handling some situations with women for the first time. Help yourself by having straight talks.

I also recall at a time earlier in my career, when I was approached by a senior HR colleague to review a global role. To be candid, I was worried and slightly sceptical about the role. I don't wish to generalise but I am aware that sometimes I can get into a shell of anxiety in any transition situation especially when one may not be clear on the way forward. He probably had taken more risks in his life and found me suitable for the role based on my capabilities. A global role with no global exposure at the onset could be tough so I was confused about my fit and expressed my anxiety to him. He helped draw out the issues that were bothering me. We worked it through by having a short project prior to me signing up, that gave me the much-needed comfort to take a leap of faith. He taught me how to take risks and I think my being explicit about my discomfort helped him understand the issues that could be worked through. So my advice is: talk. Don't assume you are not good enough, don't be shy. Men don't always get subtleties; you need to tell them what works for you at work and what does not.

As data of any gender-diversity study will tell us, board rooms are male-dominated, which clearly enables them to set the tone. If more women strive to get there, then they can become part of the system to change it. As more women get into the workforce, they can help work through the prevailing conscious or unconcious biases, alongside their male colleagues who are willing to extend their support and become a part of the solution. Men can play a key role in fostering a respectful and equal work environment for their female colleagues.

LEADERSHIP IS GENDER-NEUTRAL

Collaboration, co-operation and support from all around propel you forward. However, as I gravitated towards leadership roles, it became apparent to me that leadership is gender-neutral. It is capability and competence-driven. What is very critical to remember at this stage is that the competition gets tougher. Men don't have it easy either – even if they define the rules. When I compare my journey with my husband, I don't see him having an easier ride at work just because he belongs to the opposite sex. He has to deal with his own fears, anxieties, politics and dynamics. He may also be faced with more aggression than me. It finally boils down to your professional commitment and value creation while managing organisation dynamics.

My own experience has been that leadership is a tough journey. There is healthy as well as unhealthy competition, subtle or obvious politics, which I have elaborated upon earlier. Credibility built on past track-records, navigation of the matrix, sponsorship and support – all of this is needed to move forward by both men and women. At senior levels, the quality of talent is very good and most people have reached there because they are exceptional. They know the game and hence the competition benchmarks are at a much higher level and fairly complex. Whereas all individuals deal with this at senior levels, charting your path is challenging for both genders in different ways

SUMMARY

Collaboration in different forms is a partnership that provides the needed support for us to consolidate our experiences and move forward in our leadership journey. Key stakeholders and work colleagues, teams, managers and mentors are essential pillars of the ecosystem where we nurture our career. Managing these relationships is essential. Some key relationships to focus on are:

- Collaboration is a function of support your give and you get. The quality of this depends on your attitude and behaviour. Being optimistic and hopeful keeps you forward-focused and on track. Being flexible helps you adapt to change. Self-assurance to be able to manage the environment in an inclusive way is the key.
- Manager: Each manager is a product of what he/she has managed in the past and so educating him/her to know how *you* specifically work, will help manage this relationship constructively. Every relationship needs a bit of learning and unlearning on both sides. Give it time and trust and it does develop.
- Direct reports/team: There are individuals who may have varied views about working with men and women bosses. The best way to manage it is to get them to focus on you as a good leader. Respect has to be earned by imbibing the right leadership behaviour and building your credibility through actions.
- Peers and stakeholders: Once friends, as you move up, your peers will be seen as your competitors and might also start behaving so. Take a broader view of the situation and zoom out. Create a network of support to tide yourself over tough situations. Provide and then seek. They may have traversed a different path to the same journey; just leverage.
- Mentors: Seek mentors and look at every situation or feedback objectively. Focus on learning and leverage their advice to

crack the code. Men can be great mentors especially in a male-dominated environment.

- Charity begins at home: It is as much a collaboration effort with your own spouse. Choose your partner carefully... someone who understands your views, aspirations and respects your will to grow as well. A partner willing to share the family responsibilities, will help you balance your personal and professional journey. It needn't be a juggling act only for women. A lot depends on how you set the rules of the game with your partner. Be respectful of each other's choices and careers and be the biggest support to each other.

- Men have key roles to play in a woman's journey. Have a professional disposition while working with your male colleagues. Every society has a certain way of reacting to a manwoman work relationship. Men have been in this arena longer than women so they do or will need to understand. They can support the challenges that women are going through to make a mark, they can be the best guides available. Be open to reach out to them.

8 CROSSING OVER

future work trends

CROSSING OVER

As economies and social norms evolve, they make a significant impact on the landscape of the workplace. In these changing times, the need for engaging more women at work is being felt acutely around the globe. Some societies are at a better stage of readiness to do this, while others are still getting their act together.

As we know, women influence major decisions for their families. The new world is encouraging this decision-making to go beyond family. I recently learnt that there are now more women with driver's licences than men, in some of the world's largest developed economies. Small steps... but I believe that this will transition into an increasing trend of more women in the driving seat at work as well. Likewise, in education, women graduates have outpaced men not only in numbers but also in performance. The future talent pipeline for the world is taking on a much more feminine hue to have a more balanced way of working together. Current trends are indicative of a high level of awareness on the part of both men and women to foster this. Organisations are trying to make an effort to be more inclusive and woman-friendly. By no means is the journey complete as the larger ecosystem of social norms has to change too. This will take time, though we seem to be headed in the right direction. We just need to persist so that our future generations inherit a richer and more diverse legacy and culture.

Among the other big changes impacting the workplace is the rise of the millennial generation. The generation's women who are entering the workforce, are often bolder and more courageous about the choices they make, not allowing themselves to be limited by prevailing biases. They are now not only learning to work around the stereotypes but also look them firmly in the eye and challenge them. Social media has created the much-needed awareness and connectivity among the youth to take a stand and speak out about their expectations from society, the political system, the government and workplace. Globally, we are witnessing that not only young women, but more and more young men are also becoming conscious and are active in providing women with the support and space they deserve to flourish in.

WHAT DOES THIS MEAN FOR THE WOMEN IN LEADERSHIP? LEADERSHIP IS ABOUT...

Future of work for women, may entail new or balanced attributes for successful leaders. This may help to have more women in senior roles on the board, more women returning to their workplace after a break, more dual careers with a better understanding environment with a lot of this being powered by technology.

In the past, leadership skill sets were defined, suiting more men leaders as they have been more visible given the numbers at the top. Many of these attributes may not have been stylistically suited to how women behaved or led. With more women getting the opportunity and persisting to stay in the pipeline, the paradigm of traditional 'alpha' leadership is changing albeit a bit slowly. This is because the critical mass of a diverse leadership with more gender diversity has not been built up as yet. As the leadership of the future takes on many more versatile shades, it is up to women leaders to firmly grip the brush and colour the canvas with the shades that suit them best!

Some of these traits will be defined differently and will make better leaders out of both men and women. I have seen effective women exhibit some of these skills mentioned below, differently yet successfully, (even though these are relevant for both men and women leaders).

- Communication: In a meeting, most effective women may remain *feminine* yet assertive. They may not be as loud as their male colleagues but are able to modulate the tone of their voice with authority to get the audience to listen to them. The ability to communicate clearly, objectively and with authority, takes women a long way in their leadership journey. You do not have to always shout to be heard!
- Team Management: Due to their collaborative style, partly driven by upbringing (not to stereotype that men are not collaborative!), women are often able to take teams along well with less ego hassles. This becomes an important differentiator as they rise to the top. This makes it easier to galvanise support on the ground.
- Conflict management approach: Again, due to their emphasis on relationships, women may be prone to manage conflict situations with more empathy and sensitivity. Likewise they may not abrade others too much in a given conflict situation, thus strengthening the relationship in the long run. This balance is an effective tool in the management tool repertoire for any leader.
- Multi-tasking: There is much research that substantiates multi-tasking is key to leadership. Women are far better at multi-tasking than men. It will be an important focus for any leader as they enhance the depth and breadth of their role.
- Facilitative and integrative style: Holding a team together or families together requires an effective leader to have high emotional intelligence. A leader's role is to maximise the potential of their teams without really demanding it, but facilitating it. Good leaders, be it men or women, admit it in case they don't have an answer but they usually know where to get it from and are not shy to ask for help.

- Decision-making: In the Volatile, Complex, Uncertain and Ambiguous (VUCA) world, not all variables will be under our control and we may not always have all data available for a decision making. Often women tend to rely on intuition. Intuitive judgement depends on how you look at the big picture and tie that up with experiential learning. Both men and women can be effective at that if they are able to reflect and draw upon their intuition rather than only applying their analytical thinking all the time.

- Balanced risks: Power can be addictive. It can provide the adrenaline rush which people get used to. The urge to keep this going and gaining more prominence may prompt some leaders to take undue risks, the fallouts of these can be fatal. Some risk is good for learning and growth. However a splattering of conservatism is pragmatic and it will be the much-needed focus in the new world. This may come naturally to some while others will need to hone it. I have seen that this conservative streak does lend that balance to decision-making in the boardroom. In my experience, women tend to bring this balance often.

MORE WOMEN IN BOARDS

Recently, there has been a lot of talk about how many women are/should be on company boards. Various countries have different laws, policies or guidelines. It ranges from fifty per cent of women in the board in Nordics and Belgium to one woman mandated in the boardrooms in India. Do we need a law to make this happen? Is this positive discrimination? Does this work?

There is a case for gender diversity on boards as women bring in a different perspective to problems. The way they think and analyse a problem and consequently the solution which they come up, may be a different one. A splattering of these different perspectives will help the board with key decisions in a more balanced and measured way.

Fortune 500 companies with the highest representation of women board directors attained significantly higher financial performance, on an average, than those with the lowest representation of women board directors, according to Catalyst's most recent report, *The Bottom Line: Corporate Performance and Women's Representation on Boards.*

The report found higher financial performance for companies with higher representation of women board directors in three important measures:

– Return on Equity: On an average, companies with the highest percentages of women board directors out-performed those with the least, by fifty three per cent.

– Return on Sales: On an average, companies with the highest percentages of women board directors out-performed those with the least, by forty two per cent.

– Return on Invested Capital: On an average, companies with the highest percentages of women board directors out-performed those with the least, by sixty six per cent.

The co-relation between gender diversity on boards and corporate performance can also be found across most industries – from consumer discretionary to information technology.

SECOND CAREERS

There has been an increasing number of women passing out of colleges and business schools year after year. Consequently, there is a positive trend with a higher number of women entering the corporate world as well.

Focus has now moved to maximising the leadership potential of women and their retention at their workplace. Retention is still challenging for women at the middle level where domestic dilemmas become paramount. This is the time when maternity strikes or sometimes ageing parents have to be looked after. Rightfully, women may take a short-term career break to manage this phase of life. However, I know a lot of these women would want to resume work post this challenging personal phase. Time is not static, circumstances change and many women who may have taken breaks to attend to their domestic responsibilities like that of child-bearing, child rearing and care for the elderly, may be in positions where such responsibilities have eased out, with children going to senior schools or colleges. Hence, after a few years, they may not have any compelling reasons on the domestic front that led them to a career break. Talented career women are aware of their potential and importantly have the will to return to work. As a result we now see an increasing interest and attention to second careers for returning professionals/ women after a break.

I have met many senior women who were in challenging roles like a trader or an investment banker. At a point in life, they felt compelled by personal circumstances to give up working while in other cases they willingly took a break. With these groups, some of them crave to get back to work once their circumstances have changed. They want to contribute through their extraordinary talent. Sadly, they just don't know how! They are unsure of being hired back, they are unsure of what they can do, given the different professional environment. There are a host of dilemmas they face!

I have many ex-colleagues and friends who have or are trying to embark on a second career journey and I applaud them for their courage. Their drivers range from being financially independent to self-actualisation. In my observation, the successful ones who made it back, have exhibited the following characteristics:

- Very **clear and driven** about wanting to get back to work. Motivation needs to be strong, whatever may be the reason. This is extremely helpful given that integrating back into the work environment is exciting but also challenging so you need a strong intrinsic drive. There cannot be any half measures in this regard. Embarking on a new career journey is no different from starting your career! Think of all the effort that went into it.

- Before embarking on this journey, they had inspected the external environment and also gauged their own capabilities. Essentially, they **prepared themselves** by understanding the job market, studying the work trends, companies or sectors that are of interest, engaging with search consultants and job portals. They reviewed these against their interests and preferences to pick the right opportunities.

- They explored and sought ways to **reskill** themselves proactively so that their integration back at work can be smoother. Learning and unlearning – both are key components of success for women seeking a second career. In a career break of six months to a few years, both internal and external environment in your preferred choice of work would have changed dramatically. Any prospective employer will be respectful of your efforts to study and reskill yourself. It also demonstrates your seriousness and commitment of your intent to return to work.

- They got out there and renewed their **network**. Serious, second-career contenders reach out for support and connect with people who know them or they feel should know of their interest and capabilities. Being visible makes a statement of your availability. More connections enhance the probability of finding a suitable slot.

- They had a clear idea about the kind of **assignments** that they sought. I have had some women friends reach out for advice on how to get back to work. Some are open to anything so long as there is some professional development and financial support, while a few others have a better idea of what they want. It is evident that women who know what they want, get it much faster. Getting out in the job market and being open to any role is not a great strategy or a positioning of self and your skill set. Being open to various opportunities within an area of interest may be a better way forward.

- Many second-career women look for **flexibility,** which will help them ease into work while easing out of family responsibility. Flexibility could mean working part-time or working remotely from home through mobile apps. Given the technology strides and the onset of the tech-savy millennial generation, remote working is the way to go. However, the part-time option of a few days is yet not that evolved in the mindset of people in all countries, and corporates are working through these cultural barriers. In my view, it is far easier to make a part-time option work if you have been with an organisation for a while and have built the connections and internal equity that make this work more smoothly. I have seen a few colleagues joining work full-time for sixmonths to a year, building the internal connects, and then moving onto part-time or flexi-schedules. On this aspect, how far you want to push, will finally depend on how intensely you want to be engaged back at work.

The market always has an insatiable hunger for talent. Given that there are so many talented women searching for opportunities to resurrect their careers and relive their dreams of climbing up the corporate ladder, this is a win-win for both sides. The investment of time and effort in educating and re-training these women is yet not fully leveraged. It can be a real driving force as these women, emboldened by their commendable past careers are ready to re-enter the workforce bandwagon. Age is never a barrier for good talent, so never let that hold you back!

DUAL CAREERS; NUCLEAR FAMILIES

Smaller families and the monetary needs associated with them are forcing companies to review their support models for working parents. The good news is that most companies are focusing on how they can help with child-care, especially in emerging markets given that there is a lack of infrastructure for child care unless your parents can live with you. The not-so-good news is that not all of them have succeeded. More organisations will need to focus on flexible options for both men and women, if men were to provide support at home. Paternity leave needs to be longer than a few weeks if we wish women to return to work on time. Many of these concepts are evolving. I do witness a mindset change that is underway for a better future, where men and women share responsibilities at home and at work. Dual careers also enable financial independence for women that instils a sense of security and confidence in them. It also enables them to be financially savvy with their investments and support their families shoulder-to-shoulder with their partners.

In emerging markets, women are now getting married at a later age. The age for marriage seems to have moved from the early twenties to late twenties. This helps women to kick off their career and stay committed longer. Also, with experience and maturity they are able to gauge their choice of spouse better and be sure about how it matches with their interest. Women are increasingly more focused on support that they get from their partner and how they make things work at home, together. They expect more respect for the work they do at office and not just at home. As a family, with both partners working, I have found that one can take more risk in their career to gauge an upside for the family and pursue unchartered territories and new ideas if they wish to!

LEVERAGING TECHNOLOGY

Technology and virtual working: We would all agree that technology is a great enabler for many aspects of our life. It has been a tremendous driver in changing our work habits thereby leading to cultural and behavioural changes at the workplace. This trend is likely to continue and will foster the growth of diverse work force in time to come.

As organisations become more comfortable with work output being delivered 'anytime, anywhere', women must capitalise this opportunity effectively to their advantage. Several organisations have progressive remote working options available that can be leveraged to allow a much more effective balance between work and personal priorities.

I have however seen many driven women shy away from using these with the fear of how it would impact their careers. Perception issues exist. They think that it is better to be physically present at work at the cost of discomforting imbalance, rather than work productively from home. Sometimes, working from home may be perceived as not working! This is a sad reality in a few places. But on a positive note, I have seen some organisations, including mine, that offer best-in-class virtual, working options that can be more leveraged by both men and women.

Remote working can be leveraged intelligently, when women are in office, to monitor domestic issues. India has seen a sharp rise in many young mothers using integrated cameras at home to monitor the safety of their children over the internet, while they are away! I have shared examples of how I have extensively used Skype to actually bridge the physical distance between my family and me. From counselling the children to instructing the cook on the children's favourite recipes, I have successfully tried it all on Skype or Face Time!

Also, learning and re-skilling has changed completely with the advent of technology. People do not need to spend time in physical classrooms to learn. Virtual sessions, online libraries, Coursera, TED talks – you name it and it is available! I feel it is extremely important for women to keep their skills refreshed especially if they plan to return to work. I have probably learnt more from TED Talks than classroom sessions! Short bytes of learning can be sufficient to keep expanding our skills and horizons with very limited demand on time. It is my sincere advice to leverage these well between household chores.

The future workplace is starting to look quite different from the workplace we grew up in. With so many positive developments that make for a more promising future for women at work, it is in the collective hands of organisations, families and women themselves to make it work!

CONCLUSION
key takeaways

CONCLUSION

'You are not what has happened to you but you are what you chose to become!'
– Chuck Norris

Life is about choices and my journey till date is reflective of the choices I have made! Each of us is unique and made choices on the basis of what we really wanted. I think life is a quest for answers of some existential questions we are constantly faced with.

- Who am I really?
- What do I really want?
- How do I want to be remembered when I'm gone?
- Where exactly do I see myself in the future?

My fears, my joys, my dreams, my hope and my longings are what really make me who I am. My joys come from being myself and being accepted by who I value. Sustained happiness comes to me from fulfilment of my dreams and not only from my accomplishments. My hope keeps me optimistic, keeps me looking into the future. It propels me forward in life and helps me enjoy the ride.

As I reflect on my journey and that of others around me, I feel we all find our calling sooner or later. Maybe sometimes the journey *is* the calling! Persistence and patience are key. There are various women around me who are homemakers, professionals, working from home, and so on. There are men around me who are professionals, work to earn a living; some pursue art and some are from other fields. We have something to learn from

198 ❖ CAN I HAVE IT ALL?

each as they are made up of their unique dreams. I learnt from their collective past experience and mine and to leverage these learning for the future,

What is pertinent is that in some way we all are in the quest for happiness and pursue that! Some find it and some don't, hence my reflections as a career woman are a reflection of my search for happiness. It does not imply that this makes all working women or homemakers happy! This, however, gives me a sense of purpose and identity.

My key takeaways have been:

- Leverage your strengths and stop beating yourself down on what you can't get right. Through various roles, I learnt how to work and manage male colleagues, teams or managers but I have to confess that I have not felt any need to change myself fundamentally to successfully work and interact with them. If I did that, I would not be authentic and that would come through. It would have then hampered any trusting relationship with my working group. Flexing my style to connect with people, getting them to understand me and having them understand me was important. It was not about me being liked as a colleague but also respected as a professional. This has been the key to what I have been able to achieve at work.

- In my quest of doing various roles in a male-dominated environment, I have had to be more assertive at times and be less shy of speaking up. It was required of me to be able to express my views around the table. I think my sense of intuition, being perceptive of people's emotions and non-verbal cues, have often helped me respond appropriately in different situations.

- Learn to negotiate better for yourself. In my own experience and from what I observed around me, women are actually very good negotiators for others. I have worked with a banking recruiter and she was fantastic when it came to negotiating compensation packages while hiring bankers. She understood all the nuances of rewards structure and also had the Emotional Quotient to connect and acquire talent by getting them at the right level and pay. However she struggled to negotiate for herself especially when it came to her own pay. In my observation this is a pervasive problem wherein women ask for others but struggle when it comes to themselves. As multiple researches tell us that women get paid less than men by a margin, for doing the same job. We need to bridge this disparity by *asking* for the right value for our efforts.

– Financial independence and security: By simply working in an office or having careers and getting paid for it does not make women independent. I know some very serious career women who are uncomfortable dealing with their finances. More than often, this is delegated to their partner, spouse or father. It is important that women understand and manage their finances jointly with their partners as well. Delegation of investments and taxes implies that we are abdicating the choice of prudently thinking through the financial choices of our family.

– Join communities of support with both men and women being an integral part of it. This can be a crucial support system to alleviate you from pressures both at work and at home. Having a set of people who are there for you as friends, mentors, family, goes a long way in what you can do or achieve. It also gives the much-required security circle that most of us need to fulfil our obligations or to be able to take some decisions that may entail some risks, as we move forward in our professional or personal journey. For myself, even joining various communities, NGOs, book clubs or executive coaches, HR networks, has helped me grow, learn and progress. Most mothers will share that a network of mothers from school is one of the best support systems for working mothers, especially when one is struggling to understand the homework pages, test schedules or missed a school run due to an urgent meeting at office. I have been a great beneficiary of the school mums' network, who always understand my obligations and are there when I need them.

Alumni networks (school, college, companies) are great support systems. I have reached out to these networks very often for information, problem solving and networking. There were tremendously helpful people who were always there when one needed them for a personal or professional issue or any query.

– Mentor someone and give back. Some of us have been fortunate and privileged enough to have received guidance from various esteemed people around us. I feel grateful for all the advice and mentoring that I have received till date. Mentoring is done selflessly with a real belief in a mentee's ability. It is this selfless focus that creates an obligation for those of us who have been beneficiaries, to further propagate this legacy by giving the same selfless, unconditional support to someone else who may be struggling or looking to move forward. I have tremendously enjoyed mentoring other young, upcoming women. Every year, I have had one to two mentees that I spent time with and it is one of the most fulfilling experiences to see them grow and flourish. Also, mentoring other young, talented women has further taught me several lessons about how the new generation thinks and works. I have been truly impressed with their drive and motivation. Determined, risk-taking women entering the workforce, feels so much stronger, and it truly impresses me. By giving to others, I have gained again and much more!

– Renew skill sets/self-awareness: Caught amongst multiple and sometimes conflicting priorities at work and home, often what women give up is the focus on their professional development and growth. Women are very focused on ensuring this is done for their family, husband or children but often neglect themselves. If we want to remain professionally active, it is important that we keep our knowledge and skill set relevant to our professional context. It is helpful to do short-term courses, training programmes or an off-project at work or off-work to help build this after one has identified the gaps and areas of interest.

- Enjoy yourself. Fun is core to our existence! As I have grown older, I have realised how important it is to indulge in activities we had in school, be it sports, music, art or anything constructive. It is therapeutic and refreshes you from office drudgery when it gets too much. Many a time, excellent ideas have come to me, while I'm on a treadmill or swimming! In Asia unlike the West, time is fluid and people work longer and will happily work over the weekends. This is appropriate once in a while; however, making this a habit can interfere with family time which is extremely crucial. I have learnt from a few of my colleagues, how blocking personal time for family and hobbies, in your schedule is important to living a full life! Don't sacrifice this.

John Lennon famously said, 'When I was five years old, my mother always told me that happiness was the key to life. When I went to school, they asked me what I wanted to be when I grew up. I wrote down *happy*. They told me I didn't understand the assignment, and I told them they didn't understand life.'

CONCLUDING REFLECTIONS

I stand at the airport again. This time in Delhi, to catch a flight to London for a vacation, a city which is home to my children. I'm overwhelmed by how kind life has been to us. I have had my ups and down, joys and sorrows, happy and tough moments, but it is these experiences which have made my life so rich and meaningful.

People who matter to me – my mentors and work colleagues are there for me, and these relationships are now beyond work. It is an unsaid, inexplicable bond for life, that gives me the confidence to keep moving forward. It is extremely fulfilling to see some of your protégés and team members grow! I have always believed in hiring better than myself. The next generation is our future. It is wiser to invest in them. I feel so proud to see them fly high, surpassing all boundaries of expectations. Deep down in my heart I feel they help me fulfill the dreams that I may have dreamt.

My family! There couldn't have been a better reward than your teenage daughter telling you how proud she is of what you do and how she understands and appreciates the effort that this may have taken. I feel closer to her than ever before and will always be there for her when she starts her career or family, as I know what it takes. My husband, for his understanding and sharing the family responsibilities as he should have. Helping me make some very tough decisions at the cross roads of various junctures in my career. Parents for being there, always! I could not have done without their unconditional support. They have always been there for me and now for my children as well.

Life has given me so much to be grateful for. I am truly thankful for my joys that have kept me wanting for more. I'm toughened by my sorrows that made me stronger to weather adversity of any kind. I have it all! The ups and down of life, laughter and tears, successes and failures, friends and enemies and finally love and endless love. I love the life that is pulsating around me with all its colourful vibrance!

The last call for the flight has been announced and I rush to my gate – next travel, next destination, next challenge and more excitement. I don't know what is in store in the next phase of my life but going by the mysterious past that has unfolded so beautifully I truly can't wait to move forward. I want to keep going and have it all! Maybe I can have it all for some time and *some* of it *all* the time. But *can* I have it all, all the time? The answer is yes. If you know what 'all' means for you and not as dictated by the world, you are good to go! 'All' is that which provides you happiness and it can be only defined by you. I had it all as I defined it for myself in my journey...wish you all the best in yours!

ANNEXURE

ANNEXURE

It is increasingly a business imperative for organisations to attract and retain more women in the workforce. More and more women are asking themselves what it takes to stay at work and on their own terms. The answers to this question are not always simple. Each woman has a slightly different circumstance; hence the solutions too, are very personal to each woman.

There are a variety of social, cultural and economic factors that influence the presence and role of women in society and the workplace. These myriad complex factors shape the thinking of families, institutions, governments and women themselves, having a lasting impact on their presence and position across various walks of life.

Some of the developed economies struggle with the lack of presence of women in politics and government, while a country like India, albeit presenting many unique challenges to women, has had a woman Prime Minister several decades ago! Paid maternity leave policies in many developed economies are worse than developing nations and a topic of much debate in recent times.

The world's largest democracy, India, is home to multitudinous cultural, social and political diversity. While the world may view India as one large country, it is also known to be a complicated and contrasting nation. Owing to a very large geographic spread, the country is composed of twenty nine states (many of them larger than several countries) and seven union territories. There are twenty-two languages recognised by the constitution and over seven hundred and eighty reported languages used in the country as published by the *People's Linguistics Survey of India*! While four major religions are practised by the populace, several world religions find some representation in India. There are known to be over a thousand ethnic groups in the country! The country's four thousand-year-old history of blending cultures, compounded by an intricate web of social and cultural norms in practice even today, present a multi-faceted and almost labyrinthine environment in the country!

The country has undergone a progressive economic growth over the last century. However, the economy remains dependent on the agricultural sector even today. While the majority of Indian population still lives in rural communities, by 2030, a projected forty per cent of India's population will have moved to the cities, doubling the urban population. McKinsey reports that seventy per cent of new jobs and seventy per cent of Indian GDP will be created in India's cities between now and 2030 (***India's Urban Awakening: Building Inclusive Cities, Sustaining Economic Growth*, McKinsey Global Institute (2010))**. A vast rural and urban divide runs across the country, with the disparity widening with urban growth.

The liberalised Indian economy has created new job opportunities and contributed to rising income levels. One of India's greatest resources is that it has the largest working-age population in the world, and the majority of this population in the organised sector speaks English(Catalyst. *First Step: India Overview. New York: Catalyst, 2013)*. While developed economies are expected to undergo a decline in working population, India's labour force is expected to grow by thirty two percent over the next twenty years(' ***India Country Profile 1–95. Business Source Premier' (2012)**.According to various studies, currently, fifty one per cent of the Indian population is under twenty five, and sixty six percent is under thirty five, while only six percent of the population is over sixty five. The median age of the country's population is among the youngest in the world at twenty six point seven years.

GENDER RATIOS IN INDIA

As stark as it might sound, the gender ratio at birth itself is currently not balanced in many parts of the world. India's sex ratio is skewed in favour of men at 940 females for 1000 males, with some states reporting ratios as low as 877 females per 1000 males(*2011 Census Survey of India*).These ratios are a representation of a deep-seated gender bias that exists to this day. Driven by regressive thoughts, the practice of female infanticide exists even today and not just in rural, but also in urban areas. While there have been several measures introduced by the government to address this, biases are deep-seated and require a lasting social change in order to be dealt with. Not just in India, but across other emerging markets, gender ratio is skewed towards males, highlighting an issue that exists right at the starting point.

STATUS OF WOMEN

The status and role of women in India is thus defined by a complex variety of influences. While the Indian constitution guarantees gender equality, gender rights guaranteed by the constitution do not extend over religious personal laws, which often give fewer rights to women. Eighty per cent of the population lives according to Hinduism and its customs and laws; the Muslim population follows the Islamic Sharia code (Catalyst. *First Step: India Overview. New York: Catalyst, 2013)*. Both these religions follow patriarchal systems and women face discriminatory access in many areas such as inheritance, education and child custody. The practices are known to be commonly justified by the argument that women have no financial responsibility towards their husbands and children. While law abolished several discriminatory traditions after Independence, many women continue to live with them in rural India. Due to prevailing customs and traditions, women's civil liberties are low, extending to restricted freedom of movement and dressing.

Both the Hindu Marriage Act and the Prohibition of Child Marriage Act suggest marital age as 18. However, owing to lack of clarity and poor enforcement of laws, twenty eight per cent of women still get married between the age of fifteen to nineteen. The average marital age is twenty*(Ricardo Hausmann, Laura D. Tyson, and Saadia Zahidi, The Global Gender Gap Report 2012, World Economic Forum (2012)*. While nuclear families are on the rise, a vast proportion of families are typically joint or extended in nature. Post-marriage, women are expected to live with in-laws and extended family where they are expected to primarily play the role of child-bearers and care-takers, with the additional responsibility of elderly-care. As per a recent study, more than eighty per cent of Indians agree with the statement, 'Changing diapers, giving kids a bath, and feeding kids are the mother's responsibility' *(Evolving Men: Initial Results from the International Men and Gender Equality Survey, (2011)*.

EDUCATION

Education and awareness are a critical tool to increase women empowerment (*'What Works in Girls'Education: Evidence and Policies From the Developing World'*). There are still about 774 million illiterate adults in the world, and two-third of the illiterate adults are women (*' Troiano, Emily. First Step: Women in the World. New York: Catalyst, 2014.*). This startling statistic reveals that there is much to be done in the space of adult education for women. The situation is improving at primary education levels, with globally, eighty-five per cent of primary-school-aged girls enrolled in schools(*'United Nations, Department of Economic and Social Affairs, The World's Women 2010'*). In India, according to the *2011 census*, the literacy rate for women stands at sixty-five per cent, and eighty-two per cent for men.

There is a significant mindset hurdle to be surmounted in this space, especially in developing countries. Families still prefer to invest in a boy's education rather than the education of their daughters due to social conditioning.

Tertiary education shows significantly better trends, with Indian women now being forty per cent of the students enrolled in universities *(Indiastat, 'State-wise Students Enrolment (Total and Women) in Universities and Colleges in India' (2008–2009))*, and many are getting degrees in finance, technology and marketing (*Catalyst. First Step: India Overview. New York: Catalyst, 2013.*). Yet, ironically, having a highly educated daughter is believed to be a deterrent in finding her a suitable match for marriage!

The global statistics in tertiary education are also getting a lot more balanced, thus making it even more imperative to ensure that these educated women enter and are then retained in the work-force!

WOMEN IN POLITICS

We see a few senior political leaders in Europe and in the US, which is very inspiring, but the numbers are yet dismal. Ironically, India is among the handful of nations in the world that has elected both a female Prime Minister and President. Currently, there are some prominent women leaders in national and regional politics; however, the overall representation of women in politics is low. In the houses of parliament, women currently represent eleven per cent of the Lok Sabha and ten pointsixper cent of the Rajya Sabha ('Inter-Parliamentary Union, *Women in National Parliaments* (2012'). There are quotas for women representation in local politics and are also being discussed at the national level. As per an amendment to the constitution, village councils that manage local affairs (Panchayats) have thirty three percent reservation for women. Regardless of that, the respect for women needs to trickle down at the ground levels.

SAFETY

There are several legislations to protect women's physical safety but enforcement has been a challenge. Violence against women such as domestic abuse and dowry-related violence mar women's lives within their homes. Molestation, rape, dowry deaths and honour killings are very real threats to the basic integrity and rights of women. Late evening transit to and from work is a significant challenge in some parts of the country. These violations are sometimes an expression of power abuse. Rapes and the associated deaths are regular occurrences – though many more attacks go unreported to the public or police

SOCIAL NORMS

With a vast proportion of societies being patriarchal even today, the status of women in the society is impacted. The expectations of women, their decision-making power and independence are subdued vis-a-vis men. In these societies, the roles of the breadwinner and caregiver are also etched much more strongly, thus providing women less room to spread their wings and circle of influence. The expectation that women would manage most or all domestic chores exists even for working women, in varying degrees the world over. Prevalent religious norms also have discriminatory practices against women, making it tougher to unshackle some of the biases that exist.

LEGAL SYSTEM

A 2013 study that analysed 143 economies, found that ninety per cent of them still have at least one legal difference between men and women, which limits women's freedom, rights, and opportunities. Furthermore, even if a country has laws promoting equity, these laws may not be enforced (*The World Bank and International Finance Corporation, Women, Business and the Law 2014: Removing Restrictions to Enhance Gender Equality: Key Findings*). Inheritance rights vary for women in many countries, revealing deep-seated discrimination systems. Child-custody rights in many countries are not aligned in favour of mothers. Many countries also follow religious laws where discrimination is even more prevalent.

WORKFORCE PARTICIPATION

Workforce participation rate for women across the world certainly leaves a lot to be met. The extent of women actively involved in economic activity is an outcome of the social and cultural factors discussed above. In 2010, the workforce participation rate was twenty six point one per cent for women in rural India, and only thirteen point eight per cent for women in urban areas (*Indiastat, 'Workforce Participation Rate by Sex and by Sector in India' (2013)*with overall participation being below Thirty five per cent. Ironically, over the last decade, the country has actually seen female workforce participation dip. The International Labour Organisation (ILO) ranks India 120th out of 131 countries examined for women's labour force participation rate (*EjazGhani, William Kerr, and Stephen D. O'Donnell, The World Bank, "Promoting Women's Economic Participation in India," Economic Premise (2013); 'India: Why is Women's Labour Force Participation Dropping?,' International Labour Organisation press release, February 13, 2013)*, and the World Economic Forum rates India 123rd out of 134 countries (*Ricardo Hausmann, Laura D. Tyson, and Saadia Zahidi, The Global Gender Gap Report 2012, World Economic Forum (2012).*Other South-Asian countries also fare poorly in this regard. Asian economies such as Japan stand at sixty two per cent, Indonesia fifty three, and Malaysia forty seven per cent. The US women workforce participation is sixty eight, UK at sixtynine and Norway at seventy six per cent (*Press Search; World Economic Forum, Gender Gap Report 2010; World Bank*). In certain Asian economies, studies have shown inverse relationships between education levels and workforce participation. These statistics are alarmingly low in comparison with other developing economies with large populations such as China and Brazil.

Forty eight per cent of Indian women drop out of the pipeline before reaching mid-career, compared to the Asia average of twenty-nine per cent (*Catalyst. First Step: India Overview. New York: Catalyst, 2013.*). Career breaks for women in India come earlier due to the lower marital age and even if they don't discontinue their careers entirely, professional women In India may take several breaks over the span of their career. The Asia-Pacific region continues to lose between 42 and 47 billion dollars a year in GDP due to the lack of participation of talented women in the workforce(*'India's Economy: The Other Half,' Center for Strategic and International Studies (2012).*

The traditional gender roles and stereotypes still prevalent in India cause women to report that they have to work harder than their male peers to prove themselves, are excluded from informal networks, and face stereotypical biases against women bosses. Many also report a lack of support or empathy from their families, making it difficult to accept more responsibility and advance in the workplace. Also, with factors such as safety playing a dampener, women may often not get considered for jobs or advancements that involve travel.

Fifty four percent of companies that form the Bombay Stock Exchange have no women on their boards of directors. Women hold only two point five per cent of executive directorship and five percent of directorship positions *(Community Business, Cranfield University – 'Standard Chartered Bank: Women on Corporate Boards in India' 2010)* Global statistics on board representation highlight that there is much to be done in this space globally.

Economic growth depends on the participation of a full labour force and India's lack of gender balance in economic participation has become a major impediment in sustainable and lasting growth.

There is strong numerical evidence of a correlative relationship between women's economic participation and general economic growth. There is substantial research available that shows that greater proportion of women's income is spent towards children's health and education, positively impacting economic indicators. The Booz & Co Research – *Empowering the Third Billion*, substantiates that the economic advancement of women doesn't just empower women but also leads to greater overall prosperity.

The situation for the future is not entirely bleak – legislations and their enforcement will play an important role in allowing economies to bring more women in the net of economic participation. The evidence today is that the enrolment of girls and women in schools and colleges is on par with that of boys and men in many parts of the world. Ensuring that the girl child is allowed to complete her education is going to be an important enabler for the future.

Laws for safety of women and their enforcement is becoming an important agenda and public sentiment is beginning to create much greater awareness and sensitivity towards this important issue.

While quotas and reservation for women may not necessarily solve issues at the root level, they are certainly setting tangible guidelines towards the participation of women in the economy, at corporates and in politics, thus bringing the core issues to the forefront.

Organisations are starting to implement several measures to attract and retain women employees. Workplace safety norms, travel and flexible work arrangements and childcare facilities are positively impacting the retention of women employees.

However, I firmly believe that lasting and sustainable improvement can only be brought about by questioning deep-seated attitudes and changing mindsets.

- Barbara Herz and Gene B. Sperling, *What Works in Girls'Education: Evidence and Policies From the Developing World*, pg. 21–25.
- Catalyst. *First Step: India Overview. New York: Catalyst, 2013*
- *Troiano, Emily. First Step: Women in the World. New York: Catalyst, 2014.*
- United Nations, Department of Economic and Social Affairs, *The World's Women 2010* (2010): p. 52.
- Indiastat, 'State-wise Students' Enrolment (Total and Women) in Universities and Colleges in India' (2008–2009)
- The World Bank and International Finance Corporation, *Women, Business and the Law 2014: Removing Restrictions to Enhance Gender Equality: Key Findings* (2014): p. 8.
- Indiastat, 'Workforce Participation Rate by Sex and by Sector in India' (2013)
- EjazGhani, William Kerr, and Stephen D. O'Donnell, The World Bank, 'Promoting Women's Economic Participation in India,' Economic Premise (2013); 'India: Why is Women's

Labour Force Participation Dropping?,' International Labour Organisation press release, February 13, 2013; Ricardo Hausmann, Laura D. Tyson, and Saadia Zahidi, *The Global Gender Gap Report 2012*, World Economic Forum (2012)

- Press Search; World Economic Forum, Gender Gap Report 2010; World Bank
- McKinsey&Company – Women Matter: An Asian Perspective. Harnessing female talent to raise corporate performance
- ShirishSankhe, IreenaVittal, Richard Dobbs, et al, *India's Urban Awakening: Building Inclusive Cities, Sustaining Economic Growth*, McKinsey Global Institute (2010).
- Gary Barker, Manuel Contreras, Brian Heilman, Ajay Singh, Ravi Verma, and Marcos Nascimento, *Evolving Men: Initial Results from the International Men and Gender Equality Survey*, (2011).
- Inter-Parliamentary Union, *Women in National Parliaments* (2012).
- Karl F. Inderfurth and Persis Khambatta, 'India's Economy: The Other Half,' Center for Strategic and International Studies (2012).
- Community Business, Cranfield University – 'Standard Chartered Bank: Women on Corporate Boards in India' 2010

ABOUT THE CHERIE BLAIR FOUNDATION FOR WOMEN

The Cherie Blair Foundation for Women provides women entrepreneurs in developing and emerging markets with the skills, technology, networks and access to capital that they need to become successful small and growing business owners, so that they can contribute to their economies and have a stronger voice in their societies. Working in partnership with local and international non-profit organisations, the private and public sector, the Cherie Blair Foundation for Women develops projects with sustainable solutions to the challenges women entrepreneurs face through three programmes: Enterprise Development, Mentoring and Mobile Technology.

In India, the Foundation has worked with India's Self Employed Women's Association (SEWA) and the Vodafone Foundation in India to develop a mobile application to support a successful women-led agricultural cooperative. It is also working in partnership with the Mann Deshi Foundation to support women entrepreneurs in the Maharashtra region.

For further information, please visit: www.cherieblairfoundation. org.

ABOUT THE AUTHOR

Picture courtesy: RED The Frazer and Haws Magazine

Anuranjita Kumar is a Human Resources veteran of over 20 years and has traversed the world in various assignments. She has held a variety of senior Human Resources roles in Asia, North America and Europe. Currently she is Head of Human Resources for Citi, South Asia. Armed with her first-hand cross-cultural experience as a woman in the global corporate world and her deep-seated knowledge on diversity initiatives, Anuranjita has a keen interest on mentoring women.

She been recognised as amongst the 'Most Powerful Woman Leaders' by Fortune India in 2013 and as "HR Professional of the year" by ABP Star News & HRD Congress in 2015.

Throughout her career, Anuranjita has focused on developing commercially viable HR strategies, fostering global talent and cultivating a responsible and enriching corporate culture that believes in the progress of its people. She also actively engages as a coach for senior executives within and outside of Citi and has been accredited as an executive coach by I-coach academy in the UK and by the European Mentoring and Coaching Council.

Anuranjita is a management graduate of XLRI, specialising in Human Resources. She attended Welhams Girls School and is a gold medallist in Psychology from Delhi University. She is keenly involved in volunteering with underprivileged children and enjoys spending time with her family, reading and travelling. She is also a certified diver and has explored some of the best known diving sites globally.